PASTA MODERN

PASTA MODERN

NEW & INSPIRED RECIPES FROM ITALY

FRANCINE SEGAN

Photographs by Lucy Schaeffer

Stewart, Tabori & Chang
NEW YORK

Published in 2013 by Stewart, Tabori & Chang
An imprint of ABRAMS

Text copyright © 2013 Francine Segan
Photographs copyright © 2013 Lucy Schaeffer, with the following exceptions:

Pages 17, 37, 77, 145, 151, 153, 157, and 173: Francine Segan
Pages 18 and 117: Francesca D'Orazio Buonerba
Pages 20 and 87: Emanuele Lombardo of Eco del Gusto
Page 29: Maurizio Maurizi of La Cucina di Calythanus
Page 54: Giuseppe Perrone of Studio Due
Page 134: Sara Bardelli of Qualcosa di Rosso
Pages 144 and 157: Loriana Ponti of La Mercante di Spezie
Page 149: Sonia Piscicelli of Il Pasto Nudo
Page 161: Agostina Battaglia of My Pan e Burro e Marmellata

Library of Congress Control Number: 2013935989

ISBN: 978-1-61769-062-4

EDITOR: Elinor Hutton
DESIGNER: Laura Palese
PRODUCTION MANAGER: Tina Cameron
FOOD STYLIST: Simon Andrews
PROP STYLIST: Amy Wilson

The text of this book was composed in Freight Text Pro and National.

Printed and bound in China

10 9 8 7 6 5 4 3 2 1

Stewart, Tabori & Chang books are available at special discounts when purchased
in quantity for premiums and promotions as well as fundraising or educational
use. Special editions can also be created to specification. For details, contact
specialsales@abramsbooks.com or the address below.

THE ART OF BOOKS SINCE 1949

115 West 18th Street
New York, NY 10011
www.abramsbooks.com

Pages 202 through 205 constitute a continuation of this page.

For Angela Marchese and
Gianluca Traversa, whose gift
for friendship opened an Italy
I might never have known.
Cent'anni "bambini"!

TABLE OF
Contents

·1·
Appetizers & Soups

·2·
Fruit

·3·
Nuts

Introduction

Here in the States, we imagine an Italy populated by black-clad grandmas, patiently stirring enormous pots of tomato sauce for Sunday's family dinner. But today's Italy is a different scene: vibrant, ever-changing, and moving forward.

This goes for food too, as chefs, bloggers, home cooks, and, yes, even grandmas not only tweak classic dishes but also create entirely new ones with nontraditional ingredients and unusual pairings. In this book you'll find many of those delightful recipes. Yet one thing remains unchanged—no matter how modern, cutting-edge, or innovative—Italians universally have the almost inborn cultural sense to know when enough is enough. Their recipes tend to focus on just a few quality ingredients, so the palate is never overwhelmed.

I have a fierce, profound, and zealous reverence for Italian pasta, one of that country's most important culinary patrimonies. So, to find authentic dishes, I explored the far reaches of Italy, visiting all twenty regions and almost all of its more than one hundred provinces. I went to dozens of food festivals, which Italians hold to celebrate every ingredient imaginable, from artichokes to zucchini. I attended food shows like *Cibus*, which features the latest products, innovations, and trends; *Identitá Golose*, which hosts events with Italy's top chefs to highlight the best of contemporary Italian cuisine; and *I Primi d'Italia*, a yearly event dedicated exclusively to Italian first courses.

I traveled to locales so remote they didn't have internet access, to taste local grandmothers' homemade specialties, and met with young bloggers for what was new and cutting edge. I called on some of Italy's top chefs, cookbook authors, journalists, cooking school instructors, and leading pasta makers. I dove into the available pool of recipes, and sifted through those lesser-known outside of Italy to find the most delicious and unique.

I surfaced with some that were traditional—even centuries old—and some newly invented, like **Pasta Sushi** (page 24) and **Cappuccino-Caper Pasta** (page 137).

I found entire recipe categories that may surprise you: I've filled a chapter with savory pasta accented with chocolate and coffee, another one with fruit sauces, and a third entirely vegetarian, with recipes so delectable that even meat lovers crave seconds. There are also many vegan recipes, like **Spaghetti with Chestnuts** (page 56) and **Pasta with Zesty Horseradish-Tomato Sauce** (page 81), that are so mouthwatering they don't even need cheese. Many recipes feature new techniques, like smoking the pasta, as in **Smoked Spaghetti with Charred Tomatoes** (page 82), or cooking it in vegetable juice instead of water, as in **Purple Pasta** (page 92). There's a chapter on holiday specialties and even one on pasta for dessert. Despite these unusual pairings and new techniques, most of the recipes in this book are quite simple and quick to prepare. The vast majority use dried, ready-made pasta.

While I wanted to focus on recipes that were truly unusual, some were too out there, even for me. I was fine with—and loved!—**Fish Heads, Fish Heads** (page 110)—a delightful sauce made with heads and other fish parts usually discarded—but I couldn't bring myself to make a pasta stuffed with cow brains, like the classic *marubini* from Cremona. You will find a recipe that can incorporate cockscomb, the **Fit for a King** giblet ragù (page 119), which is the perfect dish for the rising numbers of offal fanatics, but no dormouse-and-thrush macaroni—*maccarruni con ragu di ghiro e tordi*—from Calabria and no *ragù di carne di cavallo*, a horse-meat sauce from Puglia.

I've also showcased dozens of unique pasta shapes in order to entice you to try new ones. Most of the shapes I mention in the ingredient lists are shown in the photo glossary at the end of the book. There are fifty-two different dried pasta shapes featured—one per week, if you like—all of which I recommend you try!

How to Cook Pasta Like an Italian

"MY WAY..."

Frank Sinatra isn't the only one to croon that line. Every single Italian I interviewed told me their recipe was *a modo mio.*

In a tiny town near Salerno in Campania, one *nonna* told me that her version of Cavatelli with Goat Ragù (page 124) was "vastly different" from the one her neighbor two courtyards over had taught me the day before. When I pointed out that they seemed exactly the same, she huffed, "Pfff, she uses *two* cloves of garlic."

I encourage you throughout the book to do it "my way" . . . meaning YOUR way! Feel free to add more or less of any ingredient. The amounts listed are just a rough suggestion, and in fact it is almost impossible to give exact quantities in many cases. This is especially true for foods that can vary widely in taste depending on quality or freshness, like grated cheese, garlic cloves, and minced herbs. For example, if you buy farmer's-market–fresh basil in July, it will taste stronger, and therefore you'll need less, than supermarket basil you buy in January. Aged, good-quality, imported Parmesan cheese will taste both less salty and more cheesy than pre-grated supermarket cheese, so you'll need to use less, but perhaps add a pinch more salt to the recipe. The only way through this is to do as the Italians do: Taste as you cook, and adjust seasonings accordingly. I cannot stress this point strongly enough. For raw foods, like the ground-meat mixture for meatballs, pinch off a tiny portion and either pan fry or microwave it and then taste.

I loathe tablespoon and cup measurements for subjective ingredients like cheese, herbs, olive oil, and salt, as how much you use is totally up to your own tastes, but I include them to give you a ballpark idea of quantity. Please use those measurements only as rough guidelines, as many foods, like grated cheese or flour, can vary widely in amount depending on how firmly you pack them into the measuring cup.

CHOOSING YOUR PASTA

There are two types of pasta, fresh and dried, and both types can be made with or without eggs.

Most of the recipes in this book call for dried pasta, but you can use fresh instead, if you like. For just a few recipes, however, it is essential to use only fresh, not dried, pasta, including the appetizer Pasta-Wrapped Shrimp (page 29) and two of the desserts: Almond Pasta Crunch (page 192) and Sweet Crispy Pasta Nests (page 187).

Not all Italians who like fresh pasta are elbow deep in flour, as evidenced by the many pasta shops located throughout the country. Fresh pasta is also sold here in the States in specialty shops and even in many supermarkets, both ready-cut or as whole sheets. These sheets are very versatile, as you can cut them into any shapes you like and prepare them many ways.

Here are just a few suggestions of what to do with fresh sheet pasta:

1 **Unique shapes:** Cut the sheet with a cookie cutter or a knife into odd shapes—triangles, squiggly noodles, circles, whatever. It's called badly cut, *maltagliati,* in Italian.

2 **Pretty patterns:** Gently roll the sheet of pasta with a rolling pin over an indented or patterned surface: a gnocchi or cavarola board, or any clean textured surface. Then cut the sheets into whatever shapes you'd like. The indents are not only pretty, but they also make it easier for the sauce to adhere to the surface of the pasta. Or press the dough with corzetti stamps, round stamps used to emboss pasta, to make pasta discs.

3 **Ravioli:** Use in place of homemade dough, cutting the sheet with a ravioli cutter, for any recipe like the Apple Ravioli with Fava-Pistachio Pesto (page 156) or Sweet Lemon-Marjoram Ravioli (page 146).

4 **Italian "nachos":** Cut the pasta sheet into wide strips and fry. Fried pasta, a typical appetizer in many regions of Italy, is served with salami, olives, or cheeses. In Puglia, they serve fried pasta crisps with some left plain and others filled with anchovy paste.

5 **Soup "crackers":** Cut the pasta sheet into thin strips and fry. Use them to top soups like *pasta e fagioli.*

THE IMPORTANCE OF QUALITY INGREDIENTS

Italians stress over and over the importance of using high-quality ingredients: the best possible pasta, top-quality olive oil, the freshest vegetables. It's true that many quality ingredients are expensive—there's no way around that. That's one reason that this book contains dozens of recipes that put ingredients like beans and vegetables front and center—they don't have to be super costly, even for the best quality.

Many chefs and home cooks observe that the more you cook, the more money you save on processed and prepared foods.

A few ingredients where quality really matters:

PASTA: Use only quality pasta. It is more expensive, but well worth it. Do a taste test comparing an artisan-made, imported Italian pasta to a bargain box and you'll see: Boil a small quantity of each in separate pots, using exactly the same amount of water and salt. First, drain and take a whiff. Note that the better pasta has a fresh wheat aroma. Next, test the pasta's ability to absorb sauce. Put a few strands of each into two different bowls with a little water and after several minutes you'll notice that the better pasta will have absorbed the water. Then pinch both types of pasta between your thumb and index finger. The inferior pasta will be gummy to the touch and soft in the middle, while the better pasta stays al dente. Lastly, taste each pasta plain, with no sauce. That should be enough to convince you!

A few of my favorite artisanal pasta companies are: Benedetto Cavalieri, Felicetti, Garofalo, Giuseppe Coco, Rummo Lenta Lavorazione, and Rustichella d'Abruzzo.

When making homemade pasta, you can use all-purpose flour or the classic Italian pasta flour, "0" flour.

BREADCRUMBS: For the best results, use freshly made breadcrumbs. Save the ends, crumbs, and odd bits of crusty breads, oven-dry them until crisp, then grind them in a food processor or grate them with a cheese grater. They will keep in an airtight container for months. Then just before serving, re-toast the breadcrumbs you'll need for a recipe in a pan with a few tablespoons of olive oil.

CHEESE: Use quality cheese. If a recipe calls for ricotta or mozzarella, try to find them freshly made. If it calls for aged cheese, like *grana padano* or Parmesan, choose a good-quality one with a nice grainy texture. Buy a whole piece of aged cheese and grate it just before use. This way, not only are you getting fresh quality cheese, but you also can vary how you grate it: Use the large holes on a cheese grater for nice chunky bits, a Microplane for fine, cloudlike tufts, or a vegetable peeler for thin slices of cheese.

There are hundreds of different types of wonderful aged cheeses, so try new types besides Parmesan. Visit cheese shops and ask for tastes. For robust sauces, try pecorino or caciocavallo cheeses from southern Italy.

BROTH: Homemade is best. I freeze all sorts of cooked and raw leftovers in plastic ziplock bags: bones and odd bits of meat, both raw and cooked, as well as veggies and herbs—stems, peelings, and cooked and uncooked leftovers. Then I boil up a batch of soup stock whenever I've accumulated enough. The stuff that comes in a can can't compare!

TOMATOES: Many recipes call for fresh tomatoes, which ideally should be summer sweet and ripe. When using canned tomatoes, select those from a lined can or glass jar. There is a staggering, and sometimes confusing, variety of canned tomatoes available—whole peeled tomatoes, crushed tomatoes, diced tomatoes, tomato paste, strained tomatoes, and tomato puree. Some recipes in this book call for tomato puree, which should be smooth and not chunky. If the brand you selected is on the chunkier side, puree it in a blender or pass it through a food mill until smooth. Other recipes call for strained tomatoes (Pomi has a good version); it's a thinner type of tomato puree, available in most American supermarkets. A great brand of strained tomatoes, also known as *passato di pomodoro*, is Alice Nero, which has superb vine-ripe fresh flavor and a very smooth texture.

OLIVE OIL: There are hundreds of brands, with a lot of variation in flavor. My advice is to taste olive oil before buying it to discover your favorites. Many specialty shops and markets offer tastings. Some olive oils are fruity, some are more vegetal, and some have a peppery aftertaste. The range is huge and exciting. Of the olive oils found in supermarkets, I personally like Colavita brand best, especially their Fruttato Extra Virgin Olive Oil, which has a fruity fragrance and nice bold flavor.

CAPERS: Buy salt-cured capers, not those packed in vinegar. The taste is brighter. The very best capers, large and full of flavor, come from the Sicilian islands of Pantelleria and Salina.

FRESH HERBS: If a recipe calls for fresh herbs, do not substitute dried. Buy herbs that are aromatic and remember that you might have to add more if they are out of season or left on the shelf or fridge for a while. Use all of the herb, including stems, which have lots of flavor. Rinse the bunch and then chop, starting at the top and continuing down, leaving out only the thickest ends and stems, which can be used for soups.

SPICES AND SALT: Use only freshly grated whole nutmeg and freshly ground black pepper. It makes a world of difference in taste and aroma. For the table or to garnish certain dishes like Pasta-Wrapped Shrimp (page 29) you might like to try a pretty snowflake-like salt called flaked salt or one of the many types of specialty gourmet salts infused with smoke, red wine, or bits of truffles.

Avere sale in zucca.

———

He has salt on his pumpkin.

SAID OF SOMEONE CLEVER

FINE-TUNING YOUR PASTA-COOKING SKILLS

1 Preparation

Pasta must "swim like a fish in the ocean," say the Italians. **So, use a big pot so the pasta has room to move while it cooks.**

Think horizontally when cooking small amounts or filled pasta. When making long pasta like spaghetti for just one person, Italians put it into a wide, shallow pan. You need only fill the pan with enough water to cover the spaghetti horizontally, not vertically! Cook ravioli and other filled pasta in a wide, shallow pan as well, so it jostles less than it would in deep water. If making many portions, use two pans. And to avoid breaking the ravioli, lift them out of the water with a slotted spoon instead of straining them in a colander.

Start with cold water, not hot, as hot water passes through different pipes and picks up more impurities. Use at least 1 quart (approximately 1 L) for every 4 ounces (115 grams) of pasta.

Never put oil in the water. It prevents the pasta from releasing its starch and absorbing the sauce.

Do not add the pasta or the salt until the water boils. The water must be rapidly boiling before you put in the pasta, otherwise the pasta becomes gummy. Add the salt after the water boils so it doesn't settle at the bottom of the pot. How much salt to add is up to your personal taste.

2 Cooking the Pasta

Use the time on the package only as a general guideline. The ideal cooking time will vary due to personal preferences, amount of water in the pot, and many other factors. The best way to tell if pasta is ready is to taste it. Start tasting 3 to 4 minutes before the suggested cooking time on the package.

Never leave pasta unattended. "Pasta suffers if it's lonely," says Riccaro Felicetti, president and fourth-generation owner of Pastificio Felicetti. You need to be near the boiling pot to give it the occasional stir so the pasta doesn't stick. "Pasta has been around for centuries; it should be respected. Give it your time and your attention," Felicetti stresses.

Never rinse pasta. The starch on the pasta helps sauces adhere to it, and is a thickening agent for the sauce, too.

Always save a little of the pasta cooking water to toss with the pasta and sauce to thicken and meld the flavors. Again, it's that starch that helps bring everything together.

3 Finishing the Dish

The absolute cardinal rule and single most important technique for making perfect pasta is to **finish cooking the pasta in the sauce**. Italians call it *saltare in padella*—jumping in the pan—which allows the sauce to thicken and the flavors to meld, as the natural starch in the pasta acts as a thickening and binding agent. I've added it to the instructions for virtually every recipe. It's an important step, so please don't skip it.

There is no "right" pasta for a particular sauce, but generally short pasta is best paired with thick, full-flavored sauces. Thinner, lighter sauces, like those made with fresh tomatoes, go best with long thin pasta, like spaghetti. Throughout the book, I suggest either long or short where applicable and when it truly doesn't matter I've written "any pasta." If I mention a particular shape in the ingredient list, it's just a suggestion to pique your curiosity, so by all means use whatever shape tickles your fancy. All the shapes I reference are in the photo glossary at the end of the book (see page 194).

Learn to play with fire! *Il fuoco fa il buon cuoco*—fire makes the chef— meaning that knowing when to raise or lower the flame is the key to good cooking. Adjust the heat and flame levels to create rich, multileveled flavors. Don't be afraid to add heat; just keep a close eye and stir constantly when using high temperatures. When you cook pasta risotto-style, right in the sauce, like Fish Heads, Fish Heads (page 110), remember to raise the heat to high at the end of cooking to thicken the sauce. It's especially important to finish on high heat any pasta dishes that feature a wine or a vegetable or fruit-juice glaze, like Pasta with Caramelized Oranges (page 42) and Spaghetti in Red Wine (page 87). Similarly, play with low heat. Some sauces, like Slow-Simmered Tuna, Caramelized Onions & "Candles" (page 106) are best cooked over extremely low temperatures, what many Italians refer to as "cooking by candlelight." Start the onions on low heat until they release moisture, then slowly raise the heat and finish cooking them on high for a deep caramelized flavor.

PASSIVE PASTA

There's been a lot of buzz in Italy in the past few years about *cottura passiva*—cooking pasta in boiling water for just two minutes, then covering the pot and turning off the heat as it continues to cook "passively" until it is al dente. This nontraditional technique, which is thought to keep in precious starch and gluten, has caused quite a stir on Italian Web forums and in newspapers and magazines.

Many Italians swear by "passive cooking," so I recommend that you try it, at least once. I find it's an especially good technique for delicate or intricately shaped pasta that might get broken in rapidly boiling water.

·1·

Appetizers & Soups

In today's Italy, pasta is served in all sorts of new and exciting ways, not only as the traditional first course to a seated meal. Popular in Italy is a new trend called *apericena* or *aperitivo cenato*, appetizers as dinner: an assortment of tiny plates served in lieu of dinner. Hip restaurants and bars present elaborate buffets, with many lush pasta offerings, like Gooey Mozzarella Sliders (page 32), included free with the price of a glass of wine or cocktail. Creative finger foods like Pasta Pretzel Sticks (pictured here, recipe on page 26), Pasta-Wrapped Shrimp (page 29), and Award-Winning Macaroni Fritters (page 28) are nibbled at bars, at cocktail parties, on picnics, or at the beach, or are taken to work for lunch. In fact, several of the appetizers in this chapter are so simple to make and fun to eat that I've used the nontraditional "serves as many as you like" format—this way you can easily adjust the recipe to serve one, ten, or a hundred people!

PASTA SUSHI

SERVES *as many as you'd like* | REGION: *Throughout Italy*

FOR THE SHELLS:

4 large pasta shells per person, preferably Felicetti brand

Salt

Rice wine vinegar or lemon juice, to taste

Mirin, sweet Marsala, or sherry, to taste

FOR THE FILLING:

Diced or thinly sliced raw fish, such as tuna or salmon; raw or cooked oysters; sea urchin; caviar; and/or cooked fish like poached lobster, crab, or shrimp

FOR THE GARNISH:

Lemon or orange zest; grated horseradish; chopped scallions; diced fresh fruit; *burrata* or other cheese; red chili pepper; and/or sea salt

Italy's amazingly creative two–Michelin-star chef Davide Scabin invented "pasta sushi" a few years ago by substituting pasta shells for white rice, making beautiful, Japanese-inspired but Italian-flavored, one-bite appetizers. Genius!

He seasons the shells with a splash of rice vinegar and a few drops of mirin, a sweet Japanese rice wine, then lets his imagination rip, filling the shells with any sort of seafood, cooked or raw, garnished in myriad ways. Try poached lobster topped with caviar, diced tuna, or a raw oyster—or create your own. You can fill them all the same, or make an assortment; just calculate about four pasta shells per serving and a heaping tablespoon of filling for each.

Chef Scabin loves the idea because it showcases how versatile Italian pasta is and how easily it crosses over into other cuisines. I love it because now I can make my own Italian-style sushi at home in minutes!

Boil the pasta in salted water until it is al dente. Drain and toss with a splash, to taste, of rice wine vinegar and mirin. Spread the shells out onto a plate and let them cool to room temperature.

Fill each shell with 1 tablespoon filling. Garnish to taste, season as you like, and serve immediately.

PASTA PRETZEL STICKS

{ Pasta croccante }

SERVES 4 *to* 6 | **REGION:** *Throughout Italy*

Olive oil or butter

4 ounces (115 g) *perciatelli* or other long pasta, preferably Garofalo brand

Salt

BEHIND THE SHAPE

Perciatelli and *bucatini* are both thick, hollow pasta primarily associated with Naples and Sicily. The name *perciatelli* dates to the 1800s, when there were many French chefs in Naples and Sicily, and probably comes from the French *percer,* to pierce.

It's amazing how cooked pasta tossed with a little oil and then baked turns into perfect golden crisps with a pretty bubbly surface that look just like pretzel sticks. (See photo on page 22.) They're great served plain, with just a sprinkle of salt, or you can jazz them up with dry spices like ground garlic, cayenne, or smoked paprika. I like to arrange these eye-catching nibbles poking out of a wine glass and serve them with assorted cheeses, salami, and olives. Keep a box of pasta on hand and you'll never need to buy pretzels or crackers again!

Preheat the oven to 425°F (220°C). Lightly grease a baking sheet.

Boil the pasta in salted water until it is tender, 1 minute longer than al dente. Drain and toss with 2 tablespoons oil or butter. Lay the pasta strands onto the prepared sheet in straight lines, with a bit of space between them. Sprinkle with salt. Bake until golden and crisp, about 8 minutes.

RICOTTA BITES

{ Mezzi rigatoni ripieni }

SERVES 6 | REGION: *Piedmont*

Cute chubby pasta tubes, called *mezzi rigatoni*, are now my go-to appetizers. There are so many ways to fill them! The basic idea is to stuff them with creamy ricotta—seasoned with minced herbs, saffron, orange zest, anything—then garnish with simple-to-make Parmesan crisps for crunch. They're impressive, but not fussy or hard to make.

Here they're seasoned with aromatic, decadent white truffles, scarily expensive, but a few grams of these precious nuggets go a long way here! A more economical but still highly flavorful substitute is dried porcini mushrooms.

Make the Parmesan crisps: Heat a nonstick frying pan over medium-high heat. Put a heaping tablespoon of Parmesan in 4 separate spots in the pan, creating 4 thin circles. Cook until the edges are light golden, about 2 minutes, but do not turn them over. With a spatula, carefully slide the Parmesan rounds out of the pan and onto a plate. They will be soft but will harden on the plate as they cool.

Put the ricotta into a bowl and season it with salt, pepper, and 1 teaspoon grated truffle or ground porcini. Put the mixture into a pastry bag or into a plastic sandwich bag with the corner snipped off.

Meanwhile, boil the pasta in salted water until it is al dente. Drain, toss with 1 tablespoon oil, and let cool slightly.

Fill each tube with the ricotta mixture and set the tubes upright onto serving plates. Garnish each with crumbled bits of the Parmesan crisps, a few drops of oil, and additional thin slices of shaved truffle or the remaining ground porcini. Serve immediately.

Grated Parmesan cheese

1 cup (245 g) ricotta, preferably sheep's milk

Salt and white pepper

¼ ounce white truffle or 1 tablespoon ground dried porcini mushrooms

8 ounces (225 g) *mezzi rigatoni* or other short tube pasta

Olive oil

NOTE: *Parmesan crisps make a wonderful appetizer all by themselves. You can season them as they cook with a myriad of ingredients: a pinch of red pepper flakes, dried rosemary, or even cocoa nibs.*

AWARD-WINNING MACARONI FRITTERS

{ Frittatine di maccheroni }

MAKES *about* **12** *fritters* | **REGION:** *Campania, especially Naples*

FOR THE BÉCHAMEL:

3 tablespoons butter

2 tablespoons all-purpose flour

¾ cup (180 ml) milk, warmed

2 teaspoons freshly grated nutmeg

Salt and white pepper

FOR THE FRITTERS:

1 pound (455 g) cauliflower florets

Grated Parmesan cheese

3 ounces (90 g) sharp provolone or *scamorza* cheese, chopped

8 ounces (225 g) *bucatini* or other long thick pasta, preferably Garofalo brand

2 tablespoons all-purpose flour

¼ cup (28 g) homemade breadcrumbs, toasted

Vegetable oil, for frying

Macaroni fritters are a typical Neapolitan street food, found in every *rosticceria* shop throughout town, made with any shape pasta in any sort of sauce. This more refined version, made with cauliflower and béchamel, won Neapolitan blogger Lydia Capasso first place in a contest sponsored by the Garofalo Pasta Company. Crispy outside and creamy-cheesy inside, these are a great make-ahead dish, as you can assemble all the ingredients a day or two before and just fry them when you're ready to serve.

Make the béchamel: Melt the butter in a small saucepan, then, off the heat, use a fork to stir in the flour until smooth. Return to the heat and cook for about 1 minute, until golden, then slowly add the milk, stirring for a few minutes, until thick. Stir in the nutmeg and season with salt and white pepper. Set aside.

Begin the fritters: Boil the cauliflower in a pot of salted water until very soft, about 10 minutes, drain and put into a food processor. Puree the cauliflower with the béchamel, ⅓ cup (40 g) of Parmesan, and provolone until it resembles cooked oatmeal.

Meanwhile, break the pasta in half and boil it in salted water for 3 minutes less than the package directs. Drain and stir in the cauliflower mixture. Taste and add more cheese or other seasonings, if needed.

Lightly butter an 8-inch round high-sided pan and spread the pasta mixture into it, packing it down firmly. Cover the pan with plastic wrap and refrigerate for 12 hours or overnight.

Finish the fritters: In a bowl, combine 2 tablespoons flour with 4 tablespoons water to form a smooth slurry. Spread the breadcrumbs onto a plate. Using a 2-inch (5-cm) cookie cutter, cut out rounds from the cold pasta. Gather up any odd bits of pasta and form them into another round.

Dip each round into the flour-water mixture, then into the breadcrumbs, coating all sides.

In a small skillet, heat 2 tablespoons oil over high heat. Add the rounds and fry until dark golden on both sides. Drain on a paper towel–lined plate. Serve at room temperature.

PASTA-WRAPPED SHRIMP

{ Gamberi in crosta di pasta }

SERVES *as many as you'd like* | **REGION:** *Northern and central Italy*

This is as simple as a strand of pasta wrapped around a shrimp, then pan-fried to a crisp delight. It's crunchy outside, with a moist and tender shrimp inside—so pretty and very easy to make. The only trick is that you must use fresh, not dried, pasta. You can use this technique to wrap fresh pasta around all sorts of nibbles: mushrooms, baby peppers, even little meatballs.

Top the shrimp with Parmesan cheese, garlic, red pepper flakes, or minced herbs, or serve with an assortment of toppings. They are also a terrific showcase for gourmet salts like flaked or smoked salt. The perfect finger food!

Peel and devein the shrimp, but leave the tails on. Boil them in a pot of salted water until firm, about 1 minute, then remove them using a slotted spoon.

Bring the water back to a boil, then add the pasta; cook until it is al dente. Drain the pasta and put it into a bowl of cold water to keep it from sticking. Wrap a strand of pasta around each shrimp.

In a frying pan, heat ¼ inch (6 mm) of oil over high heat. Add the shrimp and fry until the pasta is golden, then turn and fry them on the other side. Drain off excess oil on a paper towel. Serve garnished with salt and lemon zest.

2 to 3 raw shrimp per person

Fresh tagliatelle or other long fresh egg noodles (1 strand per shrimp)

Olive oil

Salt

Lemon zest

PASTA CUPS

{ Capellini in timballo }

SERVES 6; *makes* **24** *pieces* | **REGION:** *Campania and southern Italy*

What a brilliant concept! Little nests of Pecorino-flecked angel hair pasta, baked to form perfect one-bite nibbles. Though they are excellent plain, there are endless ways to fill these chewy, crunchy morsels: with prosciutto, pesto, tomatoes, shaved Parmesan, mozzarella, salami, caponata, or garlicky broccoli rabe—whatever your heart desires.

Preheat the oven to 350°F (175°C). Lightly oil twenty-four mini muffin cups (or use disposable mini cups and set them on a baking pan; do not use regular-sized muffin cups).

In a bowl, combine the egg, 1 tablespoon of cheese, and butter.

Boil the pasta in salted water until it is al dente and drain. Toss with the egg mixture until well combined and almost all absorbed. Using a fork, twirl a few strands into a nest shape and press them firmly into a prepared muffin cup. Repeat to fill all the muffin cups. Drizzle any remaining egg mixture on top of the nests.

Bake until set, about 12 minutes. Serve plain or top each with about 2 teaspoons of something yummy.

FOR THE PASTA CUPS:

Olive oil

1 large egg

Grated pecorino or other aged cheese

1 tablespoon butter

4 ounces (115 g) *capelli d'angelo* or other long, thin pasta, preferably Benedetto Cavalieri brand

Salt

FOR THE FILLING:

About 4 tablespoons minced salami or *'nduja*, pesto, anchovy, prosciutto, cheese, etc.

GOOEY MOZZARELLA SLIDERS

{ *Timballi di capellini e spinaci* }

SERVES 6 *to* 8 | **REGION:** *Campania and southern Italy*

---

11 tablespoons (165 g) butter

Homemade breadcrumbs, toasted

4 ounces (115 g) baby spinach

Salt

2 large eggs

Grated Parmesan cheese

12 ounces (340 g) capellini or other long, thin pasta

8 ounces (225 g) mozzarella, thinly sliced

Adorable little pasta sandwiches! A riff on the slider, only the bun is actually angel hair pasta pressed into a muffin tin, and instead of a burger there's a meatless filling of sautéed spinach and mozzarella. It's all baked together until crunchy on the outside and beautifully chewy and gooey inside.

Preheat the oven to 400°F (205°C). Lightly butter eighteen muffin cups or ramekins and sprinkle them with breadcrumbs.

In a small pan, sauté the spinach in 1 tablespoon of the butter and a pinch of salt until just tender. Chop and set aside.

In a bowl, beat together the eggs and ⅓ cup (40 g) of Parmesan, then stir in 8 tablespoons (115 g) thinly sliced butter. Set aside.

Meanwhile, boil the pasta in salted water until it is al dente. Drain and toss with the egg mixture until well combined and the butter has melted. Using a fork, twirl a few strands into a nest shape and press them firmly into a prepared muffin cup, filling it halfway. Top with a thin layer of spinach and a slice of mozzarella. Add another twirl of pasta on top and firmly press down, making sure it's tightly packed. Top with thin slices of the remaining butter and sprinkle with breadcrumbs.

Bake for about 30 minutes, until golden. Let the sliders rest for a few minutes before removing them from the cups.

MACCHERONI SOUFFLÉ

SERVES 6 | **REGION:** *Piedmont*

Wild! This is one of the craziest things I've ever seen done with pasta: It is intentionally overcooked, pureed, and converted into a simple-to-make soufflé. It is then served in a pool of tomato or meat sauce and topped with Parmesan cream. You get the distinct taste of sauce and creamy cheese with each glorious mouthful.

It is a whimsical, playful creation of chef Davide Scabin, who wanted a lighter version of the French soufflé, so in place of all that butter and flour, he cleverly substituted pureed pasta.

Preheat the oven to 450°F (230°C). Butter six ramekins or muffin tins.

Boil the pasta in 3 cups (720 ml) unsalted water for about 30 minutes, until very mushy. Drain and puree in a food processor or blender, adding a little of the cooking liquid, until smooth. Leave the puree in the processor until it has cooled to room temperature, then puree in the egg yolks, 2 heaping tablespoons of the cheese, the nutmeg, and salt and pepper to taste.

In a bowl, beat the egg whites with a handheld mixer until very stiff. Pulse half the whites into the pasta mixture, then stir in the rest. It will be very dense.

Pour the mixture into the prepared ramekins and bake for about 18 minutes, until set.

Meanwhile, in a small saucepan, simmer the cream and 2 additional tablespoons of cheese over very low heat, stirring constantly, until thick. Season with pepper.

Heat the meat or tomato sauce and divide it among six small serving plates. Unmold a soufflé onto the center of each plate and top with the cheese sauce.

Butter

4 ounces (115 g) penne or other short pasta, preferably Felicetti brand

3 large eggs, separated

Grated *grana padano* or Parmesan cheese

1 teaspoon freshly grated nutmeg

Salt and freshly ground black pepper

¾ cup (180 ml) heavy cream

2 cups (480 ml) meat or tomato sauce (homemade or store-bought)

PASTA SHISH KEBOB

{ Spiedino gratinato di ruote pazze }

SERVES 4 | REGION: *Puglia*

---

8 rosemary branches or wooden skewers, about 5 inches (13 cm)

8 large scallops

1 peach, cut into 8 slices

½ small red onion, cut into bite-sized pieces

Olive oil

2 tablespoons freshly squeezed lemon juice

1 garlic clove, finely minced

Black pepper

16 wagon-wheel pasta, preferably *ruote pazze,* Benedetto Cavalieri brand

Salt

Pasta, scallops, sweet peaches, and red onion grilled on a stick—Italy's delightful answer to shish kebob.

This is a wonderfully new way to serve pasta, artful and exceptionally delicious. To make this whimsical dish you need a whimsical pasta—*ruote pazze,* crazy wheels. This is a toothsome, thick, irregular-shaped wagon-wheel pasta that was invented by the Benedetto Cavalieri pasta company in the 1930s, with a special textured design that stays delightfully al dente to the very last bite and is easy to skewer.

I spent a magical few days in Puglia with the Cavalieri family, observing their old-world artisanal methods, chatting about the nuances of pasta making, and enjoying lunches and dinners together. Benedetto Cavalieri and his son Andrea continue a more than one-hundred-year family tradition of exceptional pasta making.

Soak the branches or skewers in water for 1 hour to prevent charring.

Preheat the broiler or a grill to medium-high heat.

In a bowl, combine the scallops, peaches, onion, 2 tablespoons olive oil, lemon juice, and garlic, and season with black pepper.

Meanwhile, boil the pasta in salted water until it is al dente. Drain and toss with the other ingredients. Thread a pasta wheel, peach slice, scallop, onion piece, and a second pasta wheel onto each branch or skewer. Season the skewers with salt and grill or broil them, turning them over after a minute or so, until the scallops are cooked through, about 3 minutes total.

SOUP IN A SACK

{ *Minestra nel sacchetto* }

SERVES 4 | REGION: *Emilia-Romagna*

¾ cup (115 g) semolina flour

Grated Parmesan cheese

4 large eggs

4 tablespoons (60 g) butter, at room temperature

1 teaspoon freshly grated nutmeg

Salt and freshly ground black pepper

2 ounces (60 g) mortadella or bologna, finely minced

2 ounces (60 g) prosciutto or ham, finely minced

10 cups (2.5 L) vegetable, chicken, or other broth

Here is one of the fastest ways to enjoy fresh pasta, without even getting flour on your hands! The dough ingredients—semolina flour seasoned with Parmesan, nutmeg, and other goodies—go into a sack, simmer in broth, then are cut into pieces. The result is glorious, flavorful pasta cubes.

In the past, every home in Bologna had special little hand-sewn cloth cooking bags specifically for this dish, but today parchment paper or a cotton dishcloth is used instead. The dough can be made with or without minced cold cuts. This version includes mortadella, the real Bolognese bologna, plus a bit of prosciutto, but you can omit the meats if you prefer.

This soup is drop-dead delicious, unusual, easy, fun to make, versatile . . . and did I mention delicious?

In a bowl, combine the semolina, ½ cup (60 g) of Parmesan, eggs, and butter and blend with a fork. Season to taste with the nutmeg and salt and pepper. Stir the mortadella and prosciutto into the mixture.

Spread a sheet of parchment paper or cotton dishcloth onto a work surface, put the mixture in the middle, and form it into a salami shape. Fold the paper or cloth around the log loosely—since the dough expands—and tie both ends with cotton kitchen string.

In a large pot, bring the broth to a boil. Put the "sack" into the broth. Lower the heat, cover, and simmer for about 1½ hours, until the sack is very firm.

Remove the sack from the broth to a plate and untie the ends. Dice the pasta and divide it between four serving bowls, then top with the hot broth and a sprinkle of Parmesan.

ZUPPA DI PASSATELLI

{ Zuppa di passatelli }

SERVES 4 | **REGION:** *Tuscany, le Marche, and Emilia-Romagna*

Much like the playdough you couldn't get enough of as a child, this intriguing pasta is made by extruding the dough through a potato ricer. The results are long, thick rods of pasta called *passatelli*, which means "passing through."

The toothsome strands are flavored with Parmesan and lemon zest. They liven up any broth, as served here, or when drained, they are great topped with tomato sauce. You can easily double or triple the pasta recipe, but in that case you might want to extrude the dough through the largest holes in your standing mixer's food grinder attachment.

In a bowl, stir together the semolina, ¾ cup (85 g) Parmesan, the eggs, butter, and zest until well combined and season with salt and pepper. Let rest at room temperature for 1 hour.

Bring the broth to a boil, then reduce the heat to a low boil.

Working directly over the simmering broth, pass the dough through the largest holes in a potato ricer, right into the broth. (Or if using a standing mixer's food grinder attachment, put out a platter to catch the passatelli, then gently add them to the broth.) Simmer for 2 minutes, then remove the pot from the heat. When the passatelli float to the surface, they're done. Serve them in bowls with the broth, topped with shaved or grated Parmesan.

1 cup (170 g) semolina flour

Grated Parmesan cheese

2 large eggs

1 tablespoon butter, softened

Zest of ½ lemon

Salt and freshly ground black pepper

2 quarts (2 L) vegetable, chicken, or other broth

CHAPTER

2

Fruit

SEI UN LECCA PENTOLE.

YOU'RE A POT LICKER.

Said as a compliment to a foodie.

My passion for pasta with fruit began while I was researching my first cookbook, *Shakespeare's Kitchen*, when I discovered the many sweet-savory pasta dishes of the Renaissance. Now I'm always on the lookout for fruit and pasta pairings when in Italy and I constantly pester my Italian friends to send me recipes. In this chapter, you'll find pasta paired with all sorts of fruit, both dried and fresh—berries, figs, prunes, dates, oranges, and lemons—each adding lovely color, brilliant acidity, and delicate sweetness to the sauces.

PASTA WITH ARTICHOKES, PRUNES & SAGE

{ Pasta coi carciofi, prugne secche, e salvia }

SERVES 4 | **REGION:** *Central and southern Italy*

---

8 baby artichokes

Olive oil

1 small red onion, thinly sliced

2 garlic cloves, minced

6 dried plums, or prunes, thinly sliced

12 fresh sage leaves

⅓ cup (75 ml) white wine

1 pound (455 g) *incannulate* or any long pasta, preferably Terre di Puglia brand

Salt and freshly ground black pepper

Zest of 1 lemon, cut into long strips

Artichokes, which are slightly bitter, are nicely balanced in this dish by the sweetness of the prunes and the touch of sage, which adds brightness with its balsamic notes. Plus, it's ready in fifteen minutes or less: By the time the pasta is al dente, the sauce is ready. Ah, Italy's version of "fast food"!

This dish is typically served with *incannulate*—gorgeously long, wide ribbons of pasta that are folded over and then twirled around themselves. This must-try specialty of Puglia is available dried here in the States or you can make your own (page 152). Of course, this delicious sauce is superb with any pasta shape!

Cut off the top ½ inch (12 mm) of each artichoke, discard, and slice the remainder paper thin. In a large frying pan, heat 6 tablespoons oil over high heat. Add the artichokes and fry until crisp. Remove them from the pan and drain on paper towels. Lower the heat, add the onion and garlic to the pan, and sauté until the onions are soft, about 5 minutes. Add the prunes, sage, and white wine. Cover and simmer for 5 minutes.

Boil the pasta in salted water for 2 minutes less than the package directs. Drain and finish cooking in the sauce, adding a few tablespoons of the pasta cooking liquid as needed. Stir in the fried artichokes and season with salt and pepper to taste.

Serve topped with lemon zest.

PASTA WITH CARAMELIZED ORANGES

{ Pasta all'arancia }

SERVES 4 | REGION: *Central and parts of northern Italy*

---

3 ounces (90 g) pancetta, cut into matchsticks

Olive oil

2 medium leeks

1 cup (240 ml) freshly squeezed orange juice, plus grated zest of 1 orange

1 tablespoon sugar

1 pound (455 g) orecchiette or any short pasta, preferably Benedetto Cavalieri brand

Salt and freshly ground black pepper

Pecorino or other aged cheese, grated

This dish, featuring orange juice and crisp Italian bacon, has a rich flavor with only a few ingredients. It's like breakfast for dinner!

Oranges have an astonishingly savory-sweet quality when paired with pasta, so it's no wonder that there are hundreds of variations of this combination throughout Italy. The trick is to add the orange juice a little at a time so it caramelizes into golden goodness.

In a skillet large enough to later toss the pasta, cook the pancetta in 3 tablespoons oil over medium-high heat until crisp.

Wash and finely slice the leeks, including any of the tender green parts; you should have about 1½ cups (360 ml). Stir the leeks into the pancetta and cook until tender, about 5 minutes. Add about ½ cup (120 ml) of the juice, raise the heat to high, and boil until syrupy. Add the sugar and the rest of the juice, a few tablespoons at a time, until caramelized, syrupy, and thick, so the sauce adheres to the back of a spoon, with a nice dark golden color.

Meanwhile, boil the pasta in salted water for 2 minutes less than the package directs. Drain, toss into the sauce, and cook over high heat until it is al dente and coated in a thick glaze. Season with salt and serve topped with the zest, pepper, and some cheese.

LEMON-FENNEL PESTO WITH STROZZAPRETI

{ Strozzapreti al pesto di limone e finocchio }

SERVES 4 | REGION: *Sicily*

Lemon's tang plus fennel's freshness make a light and superbly different pesto. This specialty of Sicily whirls up right in the food processor. If they don't have wild fennel at your farmer's market, just omit it. I've made this pesto here in the States with only normal supermarket fennel and it was still amazing.

Here I suggest using the whimsically named "priest stranglers" pasta, which have a delightfully dense chewiness. The name, perhaps a secret wish, dates to the days when farmers dreaded a visit from the village priest, who'd greedily devour the poor parishioners' food.

Finely grind the almonds in a mortar and pestle, clean coffee grinder, or small food processor.

Using a very sharp knife, and working over a plate to collect the juices, cut off the skin and white pith of the lemon and discard. Separate the lemon sections, cutting or peeling off the membranes between the sections.

Put the fennel, lemon pieces, and any collected lemon juice into a food processor and grind into a paste. Add the almonds, wild fennel, if using, mint, basil, capers, and 3 tablespoons oil and process until the mixture resembles cooked oatmeal, adding more oil if it is too thick. Season with salt.

Boil the pasta in salted water until it is al dente. Drain and toss with the pesto.

⅓ cup (50 g) blanched almonds

1 lemon

1 fennel bulb, including fronds, chopped

1 small wild fennel bulb, including fronds, chopped

About 30 fresh mint leaves

About 25 large fresh basil leaves

2 tablespoons salted capers, rinsed

Olive oil

Salt

1 pound (455 g) *strozzapreti* or any pasta

BERRIES, BASIL & BELLS

{ Campanelle in crema di frutti di bosco }

SERVES 4 | REGION: *Sicily*

Berries, tingly mint, and aromatic basil combine with ricotta to create a highly unusual but crowd-pleasing pasta dish. Staggeringly simple to make, the sauce is ready before the water boils. Here it's paired with pretty bell-shaped *campanelle* pasta, but it's fantastic with any shape.

Boil the pasta in salted water until it is al dente. Drain.

Meanwhile, in a skillet, melt the butter over medium heat. Add three fourths of the berries, reserving the rest for garnish, and cook until softened, about 2 minutes. Transfer the fruit to a large serving bowl along with the ricotta, mint, and basil leaves and stir the mixture with a fork to combine.

Toss the pasta with the ricotta mixture. Season to taste with salt and pepper and serve topped with the reserved berries.

1 pound (455 g) *campanelle* or any short pasta

Salt

2 tablespoons butter

1 cup (170 g) fresh blueberries

1 cup (170 g) fresh raspberries

1 cup (250 g) ricotta

About 15 small fresh mint leaves

About 12 small fresh basil leaves

Freshly ground black pepper

RIGATONI WITH RED APPLES, ROSEMARY & RED ONIONS

{ *Pasta mele rosse Cuneo* }

SERVES 4 | REGION: *Piedmont, especially the province of Cuneo*

Olive oil

2 ounces (60 g) pancetta or bacon, minced

1 red onion, thinly sliced

2 Red Delicious apples, peeled and thinly sliced

¾ cup (180 ml) dry white wine

1 small fresh rosemary branch

Salt and freshly ground black pepper

1 pound (455 g) rigatoni or any pasta

Parmesan or other aged cheese

Crunchy bits of pancetta sautéed with caramelized red onions, apples, and a hint of rosemary— incredible! The smoky bacon harmonizes with the apple's sweet acidity and the barely perceptible touch of black pepper that lingers on the tongue. The delicate sweetness of the caramelized onions and the wonderful woodsy aroma of rosemary add another level of flavor.

In Italy, apples star in enough recipes for pasta, ravioli, lasagna, and risotto to fill an entire cookbook! Grated apples can even be added to tomato sauce, as cooks do in the Trentino–Alto Adige region.

In a skillet large enough to later toss the pasta, heat 2 tablespoons oil, then add the pancetta and onions. Cook over medium heat until the onions are softened, about 8 minutes, then raise the heat to high and continue cooking until they are golden, another 3 or 4 minutes. Add the apples, wine, and rosemary, scraping up any bits on the bottom of the pan, and cook on high until the wine evaporates, about 1 minute. Season to taste with salt and pepper and remove the rosemary.

Boil the pasta in salted water until it is al dente. Drain and toss into the sauce for 1 minute, along with a few tablespoons of the pasta cooking liquid. Serve topped with shaved or grated cheese.

SAUSAGE & BLACK FIGS WITH FUSILLI

{ Fusilli al figo moro con salciccia }

SERVES 4 | **REGION:** *Friuli–Venezia Giulia*

Figs, with their jamlike sweetness, add pizzazz to sausage in this dish, building a smoky and deeply satisfying pasta that's ready in minutes. If fresh aren't available, substitute dried figs that have been simmered in a little wine until soft.

In a large frying pan, heat 3 tablespoons oil over medium heat. Add the leeks and fry until soft, about 3 minutes. Remove the sausage meat from the casings and add it to the leeks. Cook, breaking up the meat with a wooden spoon, until it is well browned, about 5 minutes. Add the wine, scraping up any brown bits. Slice three of the figs and stir them into the mixture; quarter and reserve the other two figs for garnish. Simmer the sausage-fig mixture until it is thick, about 20 minutes.

Boil the pasta in salted water until it is al dente. Drain and toss in the sauce, along with several tablespoons of the cooking water, until well combined. Season with salt and pepper. Serve topped with cheese and the reserved fig quarters.

Olive oil

1 large leek, finely sliced

2 sweet sausages

1 cup (240 ml) red wine

5 large fresh black figs

1 pound (455 g) *fusilli lunghi* or any pasta

Salt and freshly ground black pepper

Grana padano or other aged cheese, shaved

ITALIAN BLACK FIGS

This recipe is from Caneva, an area in Friuli-Venezia Giulia in northern Italy renowned for its delicious black figs. The area's climate, combined with the soil's particular minerality, creates some of Italy's most highly sought-after figs, rich in flavor and with a soft, delicious skin. The figs are characterized by their exceptionally sweet taste and elongated shape. Not to be missed is the Figo Moro Festival there each year.

VELVETY ROASTED EGGPLANT & FIGS WITH PANTACCE

{ Pantacce con fichi e melanzane }

SERVES 4 | **REGION:** *Southern and parts of central Italy*

2 eggplants, about 1 pound (455 g) each

Salt and freshly ground black pepper

1 pound (455 g) *pantacce* or any pasta, preferably Rustichella d'Abruzzo brand

2 garlic cloves, minced

Sprigs fresh oregano

Olive oil

8 fresh figs

Aged pecorino cheese, grated

A play between sweet and bitter, eggplant and figs are extraordinary together. The eggplant is baked whole, then mashed with garlic, oregano, olive oil, and figs. The resulting smoky, sweet, creamy mix is tossed with pasta and garnished with more figs.

You can enjoy this dazzling dish all year long by substituting dried figs, if fresh aren't available. Just steep them in hot wine until tender, drain, then follow the directions as with fresh. I especially like this dish with *pantacce*, which look like miniature curly-edged lasagna sheets, but it's terrific with any shape.

Preheat the oven to 350°F (175°C).

Bake the whole unpeeled eggplants on a baking sheet for about 1 hour, until very soft and collapsed. Scoop out the flesh, removing any seeds, and press it through a food mill or puree it in a food processor until very smooth. Season to taste with salt and pepper.

Boil the pasta in salted water until it is al dente. Drain.

Meanwhile, in a skillet large enough to later toss the pasta, warm the garlic and 4 oregano sprigs in ¼ cup (60 ml) oil for a few minutes, until fragrant, then discard the oregano. Stir in the eggplant. Thinly slice four of the figs and add them to the eggplant. Cut the remaining figs into quarters and reserve for garnish.

Toss the pasta into the eggplant along with some pecorino to taste. Top with a drizzle of oil, the reserved fig sections, and additional sprigs of oregano. Garnish with more shaved pecorino, if you like.

SPAGHETTI WITH ORANGES, DATES & ANCHOVIES

{ Spaghetti con arance, datteri e acciughe }

SERVES 4 | **REGION:** *Northern and central Italy*

One forkful was all it took to catapult this fabulous mix of sweet and savory to the top of my favorite fruit and pasta list. The unusual combination of dates and anchovies was inspired by Michelin star–winner Chef Carlo Cracco, whose virtuosic appetizers of anchovy-stuffed dates are fried in a batter made with panettone, an Italian sweet yeast cake with a fruity aroma of raisins and candied oranges. That dish has inspired many Italian home cooks to convert the ingredient mix into this remarkable pasta dish.

Put the breadcrumbs in a small frying pan over medium-high heat, drizzle with 2 tablespoons oil, and re-toast, stirring often, until crunchy. Set them aside on a paper towel.

Boil the pasta in salted water for 2 minutes less than the package directs. Drain.

Meanwhile, in a large frying pan over very low heat, slowly heat ¼ cup (60 ml) oil with the anchovies, pressing the anchovies with a wooden spoon until they dissolve. Add the wine and simmer until reduced by half. Add the tomato paste and dates and simmer for a few minutes.

Toss the pasta in the sauce to finish cooking it, adding a little cooking liquid as needed. Serve the pasta topped with the breadcrumbs and long strips of orange zest.

½ cup (56 g) homemade coarsely ground breadcrumbs, toasted

Olive oil

1 pound (455 g) spaghetti or other long pasta, preferably Benedetto Cavalieri brand

4 oil-packed anchovy filets

1½ cups (360 ml) white wine

5 tablespoons tomato paste

12 dried dates, thinly sliced

Zest of 1 orange, cut into long strips

CHAPTER

3

Nuts

BUTTA LA PASTA.

THROW THE PASTA.

*Said literally when it's time to add the pasta to boiling water
or figuratively to mean "the time is right."*

Italy is world renowned for its fabulous nuts—especially almonds, pistachios, hazelnuts, and pine nuts—and there are thousands of classic Italian nut-based recipes, especially desserts and pasta dishes. In this chapter, you'll find nuts not just ground into various types of pesto, but also mixed with vegetables and offered in a variety of surprising tastes and textures.

This chapter is packed with recipes sure to please you and your guests, including many vegan and weeknight options . . . so start toasting some nuts and *butta la pasta!*

CORZETTI WITH MARJORAM

{ Corzetti al battuto di pinoli }

SERVES 4 | REGION: *Liguria and parts of Piedmont*

⅓ cup (45 g) toasted pine nuts

4 tablespoons fresh marjoram leaves, plus sprigs for garnish

Salt

Olive oil

Grated Parmesan cheese

1 pound (455 g) *corzetti* or any pasta

Corzetti, round pasta discs from Liguria, are wonderfully toothsome, with pretty indentations embossed on both sides. They are terrific with virtually any sauce, which gets deliciously trapped by the pasta's rough surface, but are most traditionally served with this aromatic mix of fresh marjoram and pine nuts.

In a mortar and pestle, a small food processor, or a clean coffee grinder, grind the pine nuts with the marjoram leaves and a pinch of salt until smooth. Drizzle in about 3 tablespoons oil, very slowly, so that the pesto is very creamy. Stir in ⅓ cup (40 g) of cheese, taste, and add more marjoram or oil, if needed.

Boil the pasta in salted water until it is al dente. Drain the pasta and put it onto serving plates. Top with dollops of the pesto, a drizzle of oil, and sprigs of marjoram.

BEHIND THE SHAPE

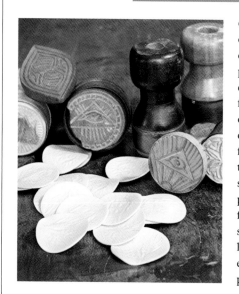

Corzetti are made by pressing a disc of dough between two round wooden etched molds, producing a round of pasta that's embossed with a different design on each side. They date to the fourteenth century and are a specialty of Liguria and the Novi province of Piedmont. In the past, the noble families of those regions would have their coat of arms carved into the stamps to create their own personalized pasta. Today in Italy, there still are a few artisans who custom-carve *corzetti* stamps, with designs that may include leaves, fruit, geometric patterns, and even initials, which are an especially popular wedding gift.

SPAGHETTI WITH CHESTNUTS

{ *Spaghetti con le castagne alla Palermitana* }

SERVES **2*** | REGION: *Sicily, especially the province of Palermo*

---

8 ounces (225 g) fresh chestnuts

Salt

8 ounces (225 g) spaghetti or other thin pasta

Olive oil

Freshly ground black pepper

*If you'd like to serve four, double the ingredients and use two pans, because the sauce becomes velvety only when cooked in small batches.

Just two ingredients! Only the Italians could create a gourmet feast using only chestnuts and pasta. The trick: The spaghetti is cooked in water right along with the chestnuts, risotto style. It's a classic "poor" recipe from Palermo that's so creamy, sweet, and luscious it's not even topped with cheese, just a drizzle of olive oil and freshly ground black pepper to finish.

Boil the chestnuts in their shells for about 30 minutes. Then, while still hot, cut them in half and scoop out the meat; discard the shells.

Put the chestnut meat, 1 quart (960 ml) fresh water, and a pinch of salt in a medium saucepan over medium heat and bring to a low boil. Cook until the chestnuts are extremely soft, about 20 minutes, mashing them every once in a while with a fork so the pieces are tiny.

Break the spaghetti in half, add it to the saucepan with the chestnuts and water, raise the heat to medium-high, and boil until the spaghetti is al dente. If the water is fully absorbed before the pasta is al dente, add a bit more boiling water. The idea is to balance the amount of liquid with the cooking time so you have a nice creamy "sauce" and, as with risotto, you won't need to drain the pasta. Serve it topped with a drizzle of oil and a sprinkle of pepper.

PASTA WITH MINT-PISTACHIO PESTO

{ *Pasta al pistacchio* }

SERVES 4 | REGION: *Sicily*

Pistachio and mint make an especially rich pesto with a lovely freshness. As an added benefit, pistachios—according to the Italians—may even be an aphrodisiac! "Wonderful in reawakening venereal appetites," a Bolognese physician wrote of pistachios in 1612. An eighteenth-century Venetian herbalist claimed they "excite the fervors of Venus." While I'm not positive about the aphrodisiac claims, I am sure this dish will get your taste buds tingling!

Boil the pasta in salted water until it is al dente. Drain.

Meanwhile, in a small food processor, mortar and pestle, or clean coffee grinder, finely grind the pistachios. Next, grind in most of the mint and basil, then ¼ cup (25 g) of cheese and the garlic. Slowly stream in about ¼ cup (60 ml) oil until the pesto is creamy. Taste and grind in more mint or basil, if needed, or reserve the remaining leaves as garnish.

Toss the pasta with the pesto. Season to taste with salt and pepper and top with more cheese, if you like, and the reserved basil and mint leaves.

1 pound *casarecce* or any pasta

Salt

⅓ cup (40 g) shelled unsalted pistachios

About 40 fresh mint leaves

About 25 fresh basil leaves

Grated aged caciocavallo or pecorino cheese

1 garlic clove

Olive oil

Freshly ground black pepper

SICILIAN PISTACHIOS

Sicily is the only region in Italy that cultivates pistachios, with the most prized coming from Bronte in the province of Catania. Each year, the town holds a pistachio festival from late September through the beginning of October, where visitors are treated to tastings of all sorts of dishes made with pistachios, including sausages, liqueurs, pasta dishes, and many desserts.

CHEAPSKATE PASTA

{ La pasta al risparmio }

SERVES 4 | REGION: *Campania, especially Naples*

I love this recipe because there's hardly any chopping or fussing. A handful of nuts, a few raisins for sweetness, capers and black olives for tang, with a hint of garlic and tomatoes—a feast in five minutes.

Poor families in Naples who couldn't afford fish for Christmas Eve dinner would instead make this dish, using dried and canned pantry leftovers. In the area around Naples, this dish has quite a few names, none of them very appetizing, like "Garbage Pail" or "Cheapskate Pasta."

Even though the hard times are over, Italians still make this delicious dish. It's also available in some restaurants around Naples during the winter, but renamed as the cheerier sounding "Christmas Pasta."

Boil the pasta in salted water until it is al dente.

Meanwhile, in a large sauté pan, heat 5 tablespoons oil and the garlic until golden, then add the nuts, raisins, and capers and cook for a few minutes. Add the tomatoes and cook for 5 minutes, then add the olives, oregano, and most of the parsley and cook for 1 minute.

Drain the pasta and toss it in the sauce along with a few tablespoons of the cooking liquid to amalgamate the flavors. Serve topped with more parsley.

1 pound (455 g) *fusilloni* or any pasta

Salt

Olive oil

1 garlic clove, sliced

½ cup (55 g) chopped toasted assorted nuts such as hazelnuts, walnuts, and almonds

2 heaping tablespoons raisins

2 tablespoons salted capers, rinsed

1 (14-ounce/400-g) can diced tomatoes

10 to 12 pitted oil-cured black olives, halved

1 heaping teaspoon dried oregano

¾ cup (67 g) minced fresh parsley

BEHIND THE SHAPE

Depending on the region, fusilli can vary widely in both width and length. The longer version is called *fusilli lunghi*, while the short, wide version is called *fusilloni*. Their name comes from the spindle tool called a *fuso*, which was used in the past to make them.

PASTA WITH ALMOND-TOMATO PESTO

{ Pasta al pesto alla Trapanese }

SERVES 4 | **REGION:** *Sicily, province of Trappani*

½ cup (80 g) blanched toasted almonds

2 garlic cloves

Olive oil

About 30 fresh basil leaves

3 large ripe tomatoes

1 pound (455 g) *busati* or any pasta

Salt and freshly ground black pepper

Homemade breadcrumbs, toasted

This is the perfect way to show off summer's ripe tomatoes at their best! Almonds impart a creamy sweetness that goes well with the acidic tang of fresh tomatoes.

Unlike most pesto, this one does not contain cheese, but is topped instead with crunchy breadcrumbs.

Traditionally, pesto Trapanese is served with a homemade fresh pasta specialty of Sicily called *busiati*, made by rolling thin sections of pasta dough around a knitting needle, which gives the pasta its name. This charming pasta shape is also found dried, available in gourmet shops or online.

In a mortar and pestle, small food processor, or clean coffee grinder, finely grind the almonds and garlic, then stream in ¼ cup (60 ml) oil. Last, grind in most of the basil leaves. Taste and adjust the seasonings, adding more basil, garlic, or oil. Put the pesto into a serving bowl.

Plunge the tomatoes into boiling water for 1 minute, then into cold water. Remove the skin, deseed, and dice. Stir the tomatoes into the pesto, reserving a bit for garnish.

Boil the pasta in salted water until it is al dente. Drain and toss with the pesto. Season to taste with salt and pepper, and top with the breadcrumbs and reserved tomatoes.

CHICORY PESTO WITH TROFIE

{ Trofie con salsa di cicoria }

SERVE 4 | REGION: *Northern and central Italy*

I love this concept. The Italians take a flavorful leafy green, usually eaten in salad, and blanch and puree it to become the base of the pasta sauce. Chicory's pleasant bitterness is mellowed by creamy ricotta with a pop of lemony tang and the sweet touch of almonds. A green dream pesto!

Ready in minutes, sophisticated, simple, healthful, satisfying, and very pretty on the plate: exactly what you'd expect from today's Italy.

In a small food processor or blender, grind the almonds until they resemble coarse sand, then slowly stream in ¼ cup (60 ml) oil and the lemon juice until creamy.

Bring a large pot of water to a boil. Wash and chop the chicory and boil until it is bright green, about 5 minutes. Using a slotted spoon, remove the chicory, squeeze it dry, add it to the food processor, and puree it into the almond mixture. Reserve the cooking water.

Return the cooking water to a boil, add a pinch of salt and the pasta, and boil until it is al dente. Drain and toss with the pesto, seasoning with pepper and salt. Serve topped with dollops of ricotta and garnish with the zest.

½ cup (80 g) whole blanched almonds

Olive oil

Juice and zest of 1 lemon

1 medium head chicory, about 1 pound (455 g)

1 pound *trofie* or other short pasta

Salt and freshly ground black pepper

¼ cup (60 g) ricotta

BEHIND THE SHAPE

Trofie, a Ligurian specialty, are tiny twirls of pasta tapered at both ends. During times of poverty, the poor farmers of Liguria would make *trofie* with chestnut flour, a staple that provided their main sustenance, and indeed the name of this pasta comes from the ancient Greek word for nourishment. They are available in the States dried, but I always buy a few pounds of the locally made trofie when I visit the seaside town of Camogli in Liguria. It's a charming village with quaint trompe l'oeil paintings of windowsills and architectural features on its buildings.

SILKY ESCAROLE–PINE NUT PAPPARDELLE

{ *Pappardelle con crema di scarola* }

SERVES 4 *to* 6 | **REGION:** *Campania*

½ head escarole, about 8 ounces (225 g)

Salt

Olive oil

2 garlic cloves, minced

12 pitted oil-cured black Gaeta olives, halved

2 tablespoons salted capers, rinsed

1 small fresh red chile pepper, thinly sliced

1 pound (455 g) pappardelle or any pasta, preferably Garofalo brand

¼ cup (35 g) toasted pine nuts

This sauce is actually a vegetable puree—healthy and perfect for vegans. Escarole, with its broad, tender, pale-green leaves, makes a gorgeous sauce that gets an added flavor boost from olives, salty capers, tingly chile peppers, and crunchy toasted nuts. Nothing is more simple and elegant.

Here, the sauce is tossed with pappardelle, which are fabulous long, wide noodles whose name comes from the Italian word *pappare*—to gobble up—but it is fabulous with any pasta.

Bring a large pot of salted water to a boil. Wash and roughly chop the escarole and boil it until it is bright green, about 2 minutes. Remove it with a slotted spoon to a food processor, reserving the cooking water.

Puree the warm escarole with 3 tablespoons oil and the garlic until very smooth and silky. Stir in the olives, capers, and chile to taste.

Meanwhile, bring the cooking water back to a boil, add the pappardelle, and boil until it is al dente. Drain and toss with the escarole mixture. Serve topped with the pine nuts.

PASTA WITH POOR MAN'S PESTO

{ Pasta al pesto povero }

SERVES 4 | REGION: *Sicily*

1¼ cups (55 g) assorted fresh herb leaves, including basil, parsley, mint, and a bit of sage and rosemary

1 small tomato, diced

1 garlic clove

6 toasted almonds

Zest of ½ lemon

Olive oil

Salt and freshly ground black pepper

1 pound (455 g) *cavatappi* or any pasta

Pecorino or caciocavallo cheese

Highly aromatic, with wave after wave of flavor—the basil hits first, then the rosemary, with a delightful finish of mint and lemon. Popular in the countryside of Sicily's Agrigento province, this is called "poor man's" because it is made mostly with herbs and vegetables, plentiful in every peasant's garden. To make enough delicious pesto for four takes just six almonds!

In a food processor or mortar and pestle, grind the herbs, tomato, garlic, almonds, and zest until smooth. While processing slowly stream in 5 tablespoons oil until creamy. It will be very dense. Season to taste with salt and pepper.

Boil the pasta in salted water until it is al dente. Drain and toss with the pesto, adding a few tablespoons of the cooking water if the mixture is dry. Top with a drizzle of oil and shaved or grated cheese to taste.

REGINETTE WITH WALNUT-ALMOND PUMPKIN PESTO

{ *Reginette al pesto di zucca e noci* }

SERVES 4 | **REGION:** *Central and southern Italy*

This simple orange-colored pesto with two different nuts is so full of flavor that you don't even need grated cheese—perfect for vegans.

My very favorite squash for this recipe is kabocha, aka Japanese pumpkin, which is naturally sweet, with a pretty flesh color and nice texture. It's the closest in flavor to the terrific *zucca rosso* pumpkins of Italy.

Preheat the oven to 400°F (205°C) and lightly oil a baking pan.

Cut the kabocha in half and discard the seeds. Put it onto the baking pan and bake until tender and golden at the edges, about 45 minutes, turning once during cooking.

Meanwhile, in a small food processor or mortar and pestle, finely grind the walnuts and almonds. Scoop out about 1½ cups (360 ml) of the pumpkin flesh and puree it with the nuts, slowly streaming in 3 tablespoons oil until smooth. Refrigerate the remaining roasted kabocha for another purpose.

Boil the pasta in salted water until it is al dente. Drain and toss with the pesto, seasoning with salt. Serve topped with a sprinkle of pepper and a drizzle of balsamic.

1 small kabocha, butternut squash, or sweet pumpkin, about 1½ pounds (680 g)

Olive oil

⅓ cup (40 g) chopped toasted walnuts

½ cup (55 g) chopped toasted almonds

1 pound (455 g) *reginette* or any pasta

Salt and freshly ground black pepper

Aged balsamic vinegar or balsamic glaze

BEHIND THE SHAPE

Reginette, which means "little queens," are one of a group of pasta named after Italy's royalty, which includes *regine*—queens—and also *mafalde*, after Princess Mafalda, daughter of Victor Emanuel III. *Tripolini* are a thinner version with ruffles on only one side, evocative of a queen's crown.

RADIATORE WITH RADICCHIO, BEER & HAZELNUTS

{ Radiatore con birra e radicchio }

SERVES 4 | **REGION:** *Veneto*

I tasted this unusual beer-pasta combination at the annual food festival in Umbria called *I Primi d'Italia*, which celebrates Italy's first-course dishes. Unique and flavorful, the radicchio rosso di Treviso, affectionately called *il fiore che si mangia*—the flower that you eat—marries perfectly with the beer's slightly bitter notes. Sautéed leeks add a subtle sweetness to this dish and hazelnuts give it crunch. I love it with the pale blonde Italian ale called *bionda*, but any beer you enjoy drinking would be fine.

In a sauté pan large enough to later toss the pasta, heat ¼ cup (60 ml) oil over high heat and cook the leeks until golden, about 5 minutes. Pour in the beer, scraping up any brown bits with a wooden spoon. Add the radicchio, reserving a little for use later as garnish, and cook until it is soft, about 2 minutes. Season with salt and pepper.

Boil the pasta in salted water until it is al dente. Drain and add to the sauce along with a little more beer, if the mixture is dry. Toss the pasta in the sauce until well combined, then stir in grated or shaved cheese to taste. Serve topped with the reserved raw radicchio and hazelnuts.

Olive oil

1 large leek, thinly sliced

¾ cup (180 ml) beer, such as bionda

1 small head radicchio, very finely sliced

Salt and freshly ground black pepper

1 pound (455 g) *radiatore* or any short pasta

Parmesan or other aged cheese

⅓ cup (40 g) chopped toasted hazelnuts

BEHIND THE SHAPE

Radiatore, radiators, is a pasta shape created after the invention of the car. Other Machine Age–inspired shapes are: *ruote,* wheels; *eliche,* propellers; *trivelle,* industrial drills; and *dischi volanti,* flying saucers.

·4·

Vegetarian

NON FARTI INFINOCCHIARE.

DON'T LET YOURSELF BE FENNELED.

*A common expression in Italy meaning "don't be tricked." It comes from
the fact that it's hard to fully taste wine while eating fennel, so disreputable
winemakers serve it to their clients to mask an inferior vintage.*

Italy, especially Southern Italy, is renowned for its many vegetable-based pasta
dishes. In this chapter, you'll discover traditional but unusual dishes like Pasta
with Zesty Horseradish-Tomato Sauce (page 81), a specialty of Puglia, which
is topped with freshly grated horseradish instead of cheese. There are also
many modern creations, including Kamut Spaghetti with Bean "Meatballs"
(page 86) and my personal favorite, Zucchini-Glazed Pasta (page 89). There
are sauces made with everything from Jerusalem artichokes to pumpkins, as
well as those made just from reduced wine, like Sicily's Spaghetti in Red Wine
(page 87) and Liguria's Pasta in White Wine (page 73).

PUMPKIN CARBONARA WITH PACCHERI

{ Paccheri alla carbonara }

SERVES 4 | **REGION:** *Central and southern Italy*

1 large onion, thinly sliced

Olive oil

2 cups (230 g) diced, seeded, and peeled kabocha or butternut squash

Salt and freshly ground black pepper

2 large egg yolks

Pecorino or other aged cheese

1 pound (455 g) *paccheri* or any short, thick pasta

It would be difficult to improve on that magical combination of simple ingredients in classic carbonara, but this version just might sway your loyalties. Sweet caramelized onions and squash take the place of pancetta, adding an autumnal note plus even more creaminess. When the weather turns cool, you're sure to find yourself making this again and again. If you like, you can plate this chubby tube pasta upright, what they call "on their feet" in Italy.

In a large sauté pan over medium heat, warm 2 tablespoons oil and cook the onions until they are very soft, about 8 minutes. Raise the heat to high and continue cooking until the onions are golden and caramelized, about 4 more minutes. Remove the onions from the pan and set aside.

In the same pan, add another 1 or 2 tablespoons and fry the squash until tender and golden at the edges, about 8 minutes. Return the onions to the pan, season with salt and pepper, and keep warm.

In a large serving bowl, beat the yolks with pepper and 2 heaping tablespoons grated cheese.

Boil the pasta in salted water until it is al dente. Drain and toss in the egg mixture, stirring until creamy, then stir in the hot onion-squash mixture. Serve topped with grated or shaved cheese.

BEHIND THE SHAPE

Italians from Campania and Calabria squabble over which region first invented the huge tube pasta called *paccheri*. The name *paccheri* is said to come from the Neapolitan dialect for the sound these wide pasta tubes make when plopped onto a plate—*slap!* You'll also find this toothsome pasta sold by the name *schiaffone*, for the nondialect word for slap. It's also sometimes even called by the whimsical name *maniche di frate*, monk's sleeves.

CHEESY DITALINI WITH FAVA BEANS

{ Favò }

SERVES 6 | **REGION:** *Valle d'Aosta*

1 cup (150 g) shelled fava beans (about 1½ pounds/680 g in pods)

7 tablespoons (100 g) butter

3 slices whole-grain bread, cut into cubes

2 large shallots, thinly sliced in rounds

4 large ripe tomatoes, peeled, seeded, and diced

⅓ cup (75 ml) tomato paste

12 ounces (340 g) *ditalini* or other short tube pasta

4 ounces (115 g) fontina cheese, diced

Salt and freshly ground black pepper

I love the earthy, nutty flavor in this dish of the fresh fava beans in combination with the crunchy bread bits and creamy fontina cheese. Made with small tube pasta called *ditalini,* little thimbles, this is one of the few pasta dishes from Valle d'Aosta, the northernmost Italian region, which specializes more in polenta and rice.

This recipe is a specialty of Ozein, a small town that each year hosts *La Sagra della Favò,* a festival in honor of this luscious dish.

In a large saucepan, boil the beans in salted water for about 2 minutes, until they float to the top. Remove them using a slotted spoon, reserving the cooking water. Peel the beans and set aside.

Meanwhile, in a saucepan, heat the butter over high heat until golden, then add the bread and, shaking the pan while it cooks, toast it on all sides. Remove the bread and set aside. In the same pan over medium-high heat, cook the shallots until soft, adding a little more butter if needed, about 10 minutes. Add the tomatoes, tomato paste, and beans and cook about 5 minutes.

Bring the reserved bean water to a boil and add the pasta, cooking until it is al dente. Drain and add to the sauce with a few tablespoons of the cooking liquid, stirring until well combined. Add the cheese and stir until it is completely melted. Season to taste with salt and pepper. Serve topped with the toasted bread.

PASTA IN WHITE WINE

{ Pasta alla deficeira }

SERVES 4 | REGION: *Liguria*

Cooking pasta in wine instead of water creates an amazingly aromatic sauce. The flavor of the wine really stands out, so be sure to pick one with pronounced fruity taste and crisp acidity, like Soave or Pinot Grigio.

Traditionally, this dish was prepared at the height of the oil-pressing season, offered by the olive growers as a gesture of celebration to those who helped with the harvest. The name of the dish is from the Ligurian dialect for olive press, *deficeira*, and fittingly, it's served with olive oil. A nice choice is the delicate, fruity variety made from the tiny *taggiasca* olives of Liguria.

1 (750-ml) bottle dry, fruity white wine

2 bay leaves

12 ounces (340 g) penne or any short tube pasta

Olive oil

Salt and freshly ground black pepper

Crescenza or any aged cheese

In a large saucepan, bring the wine and bay leaves to a boil. Add the pasta, lower the heat to a low boil, and cook, loosely covered, until the wine is absorbed and the pasta is al dente, about 20 minutes. Add more wine or hot water a little at a time if the pasta seems to be getting dry, or if it is too wet when almost al dente, raise the heat to high to burn off the remaining liquid and alcohol. Stir in 3 to 4 tablespoons oil and season with salt and pepper. Serve topped with grated or shaved cheese.

WINE AS PASTA SAUCE

In several regions, Italians add a splash of wine, instead of sauce, to cooked pasta. In the winter, local farmers even enjoy a sort of liquid pasta drink as a pick-me-up, made from the hot pasta cooking water mixed with red wine and generous amounts of crushed black or red pepper. In Piedmont and Emilia-Romagna, it's common, especially for the older generations, to top *plin*, the area's small ravioli, with red wine. In Molise, they make a simple pasta soup called *scattone*, where the broth is just the pasta's cooking water seasoned with red wine and pepper. A fabulous medieval festival called *La Sagra dello Scattone* is dedicated to this centuries-old dish, held each year in August in the Molise towns of Torella del Sannio and Bagnoli del Trigno.

BUCATINI DOME

{ Cupola di bucatini }

SERVES 8 | REGION: *Campania and Sicily*

14 tablespoons (200 g) butter

5 to 6 small zucchini, minced

3 medium carrots, minced

12 ounces (340 g) haricots verts or very thin string beans, minced

1¼ pounds (570 g) *bucatini* or *perciatelli*, preferably Garofalo brand

2 large eggs, beaten

Grated pecorino cheese

Freshly ground black pepper

12 ounces (340 g) deli-sliced high-quality provolone or caciocavallo cheese

It's hard to top this dish for pure, showstopping drama. The stately dome of pasta houses a colorful filling of string beans, carrots, zucchini, and plenty of rich Italian cheese. But don't get intimidated. This architecturally magnificent—and delicious—dish is actually quite easy to create. The trick is to use *bucatini*: long, thick pasta that keeps its shape as you coil it into a bowl.

This recipe dates to eighteenth-century Naples, and was taught to me at the Garofalo pasta factory, right in their office kitchen.

Preheat the oven to 350°F (175°C). Very generously butter an 8- to 9-inch (20- to 23-cm) dome-shaped ovensafe container, such as a Pyrex or metal bowl.

In a large sauté pan, heat 2 tablespoons of the butter and add the zucchini; fry until it is soft. Put the zucchini into a large bowl. In the same pan, heat another 1 tablespoon of the butter and cook the carrots and string beans over low heat, covered, until they are tender, adding a few drops of water, if needed. Stir them into the bowl with the zucchini until well combined. Set aside 1 cup of this vegetable mixture as garnish.

Boil the pasta in salted water for two thirds of the time the package directs. Drain and divide, putting three fourths of the pasta into the large bowl of vegetables and the remaining one fourth into a small bowl. Add 2 tablespoons of the butter to the small bowl, toss, and set aside; it will be used for the outer part of the dome.

Add the remaining 9 tablespoons (130 g) butter to the pasta-vegetable bowl and stir until the butter melts, then stir in the eggs, ½ cup (50 g) of pecorino, and a pinch of pepper. Using kitchen scissors, cut into the pasta mixture so it is broken up a little. Set aside.

recipe continues

Using one strand from the plain buttered pasta, start in the center of the prepared domed container and twirl the pasta around itself to form a coil (**image #1**). Continue the coil with another strand of pasta, starting where the last strand ended so it is in one continuous line; continue with additional strands until the pasta reaches halfway up the pan. Line the pasta with slices of the provolone, pressing the cheese firmly against the pasta (**image #2**). Put in half of the vegetable-pasta mixture, pressing firmly into the bottom and sides of the bowl to remove any air pockets and densely pack the filling (**image #3**). This is the key to getting a nice compact dome that stays together when sliced. Top with cheese slices.

Continue coiling the plain pasta around the dome to the top (**image #4**). Line the sides with more cheese slices and top with the remaining vegetable-pasta mixture and slices of cheese. Press the pasta down firmly with a spatula or wooden spoon. Cut the remaining plain buttered pasta with scissors and press it on top of the mixture (**image #5**).

Cover the bowl with aluminum foil and bake for 15 minutes, then remove the foil and bake, uncovered, for another 15 minutes, or until the pasta is golden and set. Let it rest for 10 minutes, then put a serving plate on top of the bowl and invert it. Hit the bowl with a wooden spoon to help the pasta release and, using the tip of a spoon or butter knife along the bottom edge of the bowl, carefully remove the bowl from the pasta (**image #6**). Serve garnished with the reserved cup of minced vegetables.

FARRO PASTA WITH JERUSALEM ARTICHOKES

{ *Pasta ai topinambur* }

SERVES 4 | REGION: *Piedmont*

Olive oil

1 large onion, thinly sliced

5 large Jerusalem artichokes

1 pound (455 g) long or short farro pasta, preferably Felicetti brand

3 to 4 tablespoons toasted pine nuts

Parmesan or other aged cheese

Jerusalem artichokes arrived in Italy in the 1600s, and like the other New World foods—corn, tomatoes, and chocolate—they were quickly incorporated into fabulous regional dishes. Jerusalem artichokes are especially popular in Piedmont, where they are a key ingredient in the area's famed *bagna cauda*, as well as in many risotto and pasta dishes. In this dish, the Jerusalem artichoke's sweet, nutty flavor pairs well with hearty whole-grain pasta made with farro.

In a large skillet, warm 2 tablespoons of the oil and cook the onions until golden, about 12 minutes. Meanwhile, scrub the artichokes with a brush, then thinly slice them. Add them to the onions and cook over very low heat until they are very soft, about 10 minutes.

Boil the pasta in salted water until it is al dente. Drain.

In a food processor, puree the onion mixture with 2 tablespoons oil until smooth. Return the puree to the pan and toss it with the pasta for a minute or two, adding a little cooking water if it is dry. Serve topped with the pine nuts and shaved or grated cheese.

A VEGGIE BY ANY OTHER NAME

According to the *Oxford English Dictionary*, the term *Jerusalem artichoke* is thought to be a corruption of the Italian *girasole articiocco*, sunflower artichoke. It was so called because the tuber tastes like artichoke and its flower resembles sunflowers. In Italy, Jerusalem artichokes are called everything from *patata del Canada*, Canadian potatoes, to *pera di terra*, pears from the ground, or *tarufala bastarda*, bastard truffles. The most common name for them in Italy is *topinambur*, after a Brazilian Indian tribe called Topinamboux that happened to be in Europe about the same time the vegetables were arriving. The plant was erroneously thought to have originated in Brazil as well. In Piedmont, they're also called *ciapinabò* and there's a fun three-day festival, *la sagra del ciapinabò*, every year in the Piedmont town of Carignano, just a bit south of Turin, where you can taste hundreds of Jerusalem artichoke recipes and party with the locals until midnight.

"STRINGS" & STRING BEANS

{ Spaghetti e fagiolini }

SERVES *4 to 6* | **REGION:** *Tuscany and Sicily*

Homey comfort food—try it once and you'll want to make it over and over again. It's ridiculously simple, despite being from one of Italy's most accomplished chefs: Fabbio Picchi of Cibreo, in Florence. String beans, tomatoes, onions, and garlic are simmered until very soft and savory, then tossed with "little strings," aka spaghetti.

Put the beans, tomatoes, onions, ½ cup (120 ml) oil, garlic, and a pinch of pepper flakes in a large saucepan. Bring them to a simmer on medium-low heat, covered, and cook until the beans are very soft, almost falling apart, about 50 minutes. Let the mixture cool to room temperature so all the flavors can meld. Stir most of the parsley into the sauce, and season to taste with salt.

Boil the spaghetti in salted water until it is al dente and drain. Toss into the sauce and top with shaved or grated cheese and the rest of the minced parsley.

1 pound (455 g) very thin string beans or haricots verts

1 (14-ounce/400-g) can diced tomatoes

1 large red onion, very thinly sliced

Olive oil

2 garlic cloves, minced

Red pepper flakes

1 heaping cup (100 g) minced fresh parsley, stems included

Salt

1 pound (455 g) spaghetti or any pasta

Parmesan or other aged cheese

PASTA WITH ZESTY HORSERADISH-TOMATO SAUCE

{ Pasta al ferretto al rafano }

SERVES 4 | REGION: *Basilicata*

Horseradish on pasta? I was dubious, and figured my Italian friends were pulling my leg when they told me what I'd be eating.

But no—it's real. In Basilicata, they have been topping pasta with grated horseradish for centuries. Despite my skepticism, I was amazed to find that horseradish adds a marvelous brightness. The horseradish must be fresh, not jarred, grated right onto each person's dish at the table, just like you'd do with cheese.

Traditionally, this dish is served with *pasta al ferretto*, named after the metal rod the dough was rolled around. It's available dried in the States, or you can substitute homemade "knitting needle" pasta (page 160), but the recipe is fabulous with any shape, size, or type of pasta!

Plunge the tomatoes into boiling water for a few seconds, then remove them with a slotted spoon. Peel, deseed, and dice the tomatoes.

In a wide saucepan over medium-high heat, warm 3 tablespoons oil and cook the onions until very soft, about 5 minutes. Stir the tomatoes into the onions and cook, covered, on very low heat for about 20 minutes.

Meanwhile, combine the breadcrumbs, walnuts, and 2 tablespoons oil in a small nonstick pan, and cook on medium-high heat until the breadcrumbs are dark golden. Set aside.

Boil the pasta in salted water until it is al dente. Drain and stir into the tomato sauce until well combined, adding a few tablespoons of the pasta cooking water if needed. Sprinkle with the walnut-breadcrumb mixture and serve. Top with a tablespoon or two of fresh horseradish grated on a cheese grater.

1 pound (455 g) fresh tomatoes

1 sweet onion, finely minced

Olive oil

⅓ cup (37 g) homemade coarsely ground breadcrumbs, toasted

⅓ cup (40 g) coarsely chopped walnuts

1 pound (455 g) *pasta al ferretto* or any pasta

Fresh horseradish

SMOKED SPAGHETTI WITH CHARRED TOMATOES

{ *Spaghetti affumicati con pomodorini grigliati* }

SERVES 4 | **REGION:** *Northern and central Italy*

Olive oil

8 baby Roma or plum tomatoes, cut in half

2 garlic cloves, minced

1 pound (455 g) spaghetti, preferably Benedetto Cavalieri brand

Salt

Several untreated wood chips or dry twigs

Fresh herbs, minced, such as parsley, basil, and oregano

Parmesan or other aged cheese

Some of Italy's most innovative chefs are smoking pasta these days, a technique that adds a rich layer of flavor. Here's a fabulously simple way to do it at home, without a smoker or other complicated equipment. You'll love the technique!

The smoked pasta itself is so tasty that you'll be tempted to eat it by the fistful, even without sauce. But you'll love this sauce, which delivers the flavor of slow oven-roasted tomatoes, but without turning on the oven! The tomatoes are seared in a very hot skillet until charred on the cut side, then turned over, covered, and left to pan roast.

Heat a heavy iron skillet until very hot, add 1 tablespoon oil (it will smoke) and put in the tomatoes, cut sides down. Cook on very high heat until the tomatoes are blackened. Turn them over with a spatula, and char them on the skin sides. Sprinkle the garlic over the tomatoes, drizzle with 2 more tablespoons oil, remove from the heat, and cover.

Boil the spaghetti in salted water until it is al dente. While the pasta is cooking, put a scattering of wood chips or a few bits of dry twigs in a large high-rimmed baking pan, top with a grill rack, and light the wood so the chips begin to smoke. Drain the pasta and spread it over the grill rack. Cover the pan tightly with aluminum foil so the smoke flavor can absorb into the pasta, about 4 minutes.

Peel away and discard the skin from the tomato halves—it should separate easily. Gently toss the smoked pasta into the skillet with the tomatoes and season with salt. Serve topped with a drizzle of olive oil, fresh herbs, and shaved or grated cheese.

PASTA WITHOUT WATER

{ Pasta senz'acqua }

SERVES **6** | REGION: *Abruzzo and Puglia*

I love recipes like this one, where you pop raw ingredients into the oven, walk away, and return to a gourmet dinner!

It's called "pasta without water," because instead of cooking the pasta in boiling water, the uncooked pasta is layered with sliced tomatoes, potatoes, and herbs and baked into deliciousness. It absorbs lots of flavor as it melds with the other ingredients!

It's a casual, easy-to-assemble recipe that lends itself to improvisation. Use any type of potato you like: colorful and tasty Yukon golds, purple potatoes, tiny red potatoes. Add veggies like zucchini or spinach, herbs like thyme or marjoram, and even salami, if you like.

Preheat the oven to 350°F (175°C).

In a Dutch oven or roasting pan over medium-high heat, drizzle 2 tablespoons oil. Scatter the onions over the entire bottom of the pan, sprinkle with oregano and basil to taste, and cook for about 5 minutes, until softened. Top with a layer of potatoes, pressing down firmly and evenly. Drizzle on about 3 more tablespoons oil, oregano to taste, the garlic, and salt to taste. Top with half the tomatoes, then scatter on the raw pasta. Drizzle with 2 more tablespoons oil and basil to taste. End with a layer of tomatoes, skin side up. Using a spatula, press all the layers down very firmly, all the while cooking it over medium-high heat.

Pour the hot stock over the top, put aluminum foil right onto the surface of the food, and cover it with a lid. Bake until the pasta and potatoes are tender, about 1½ hours, checking periodically to see if more liquid is needed (if it is, add some boiling water).

Increase the oven temperature to 475°F (245°C). Remove the lid and foil, sprinkle with the black pepper and ½ cup of grated cheese, and bake for an additional 10 minutes, or until golden on top. Serve with more shaved or grated cheese on the side.

Olive oil

2 large red onions, thinly sliced

Dried oregano

Dried basil

3 pounds (1.4 kg) potatoes, any type, peeled and thinly sliced

4 garlic cloves, finely minced

Salt

4 pounds (1.8 kg) baby Roma or plum tomatoes, cut in half or quarters

1 pound (455 g) *pennoni* or other tube pasta

3 cups hot vegetable stock

Freshly ground black pepper

Grana padano, pecorino, or any aged cheese

1 pound (455 g) potatoes, any type,
peeled and diced

Olive oil

3 garlic cloves, crushed

8 ounces (225 g) spaghetti, broken
into bite-sized pieces

Grated pecorino or other aged
cheese

⅓ cup (30 g) finely minced fresh
parsley leaves and stems

1 small dried red chile pepper,
minced

Salt

Freshly ground black pepper

PASTA & POTATOES

You might think that combining two
starches—pasta and potatoes—is a
little weird, but in Italy it's actually
quite common. In fact, pesto
Genovese, Liguria's famous basil and
pine nut pesto, is traditionally served
with pasta cooked with string beans
and sliced potatoes.

RISOTTO-STYLE SPAGHETTI
WITH POTATOES

{ *Pasta spezzata con crema di patate* }

SERVES 4 | REGION: *Campania, Naples*

Neapolitans consider this dish a sure cure for insomnia! No need
to count sheep when you can sup on the fluffy white clouds of this
satisfying dish. A good night's sleep is guaranteed.

Creamy, but made without cream, potato and garlic dissolve
into velvety delight. The pasta cooks right in the sauce like risotto, a
technique called *risottare*. This dish is traditionally made with a mix of
all sorts of different pasta shapes, which is nowadays sold ready-mixed
in one package. Of course, you can use just one type, like broken-up
spaghetti, if you prefer.

I learned to make this dish from my friend Sonia Piscicelli, whose
blog, Il Pasto Nudo, is one of my favorites. I love her tip to use *all* the
parsley when cooking, including the flavorful stems!

In a medium saucepan over medium heat, combine the potatoes, ¼ cup (60 ml) oil,
and the garlic and cook, stirring occasionally, until the potatoes start to break up a
bit, about 10 minutes. Add about 2 cups hot water, just enough to cover the potatoes
by ½ inch (12 mm). Raise the heat, bring everything to a boil, then lower the heat
and simmer until the potatoes are very soft, about 10 minutes more. Add the pasta and
stir until combined; simmer until the pasta is almost al dente. Stir in ⅓ cup (40 g)
of cheese, the parsley, and the chile pepper to taste, and cook for another minute,
adding hot water or olive oil if needed. Season to taste with salt.

Serve topped with more cheese and an additional sprinkle of parsley, chile,
and pepper.

KAMUT SPAGHETTI WITH BEAN "MEATBALLS"

{ *Spaghetti di kamut con polpettine di fagioli borlotti* }

SERVES 4 | REGION: *Calabria, Abruzzo, and southern Italy*

1 heaping cup (about 250 ml) shelled fresh *borlotti* or cranberry beans

3 tablespoons homemade breadcrumbs, toasted

Grated Parmesan cheese

1 large egg

1 teaspoon dried oregano

½ teaspoon garlic powder

Salt and freshly ground black pepper

Olive oil

1 onion, very finely minced

1 (28-ounce/800-g) can tomato puree

1 pound (455 g) kamut or whole-wheat spaghetti

A few fresh basil leaves, shredded

In southern Italy, beans often used to be called "poor man's meat." Nowadays, we've come to realize just how healthy and delicious all those so-called "poor" foods can be.

I love these "meatballs," which are made from mashed beans seasoned with grated cheese and breadcrumbs. The nice grain flavor of the bread mixed with the rich creaminess of the beans makes an amazingly light, healthy, and delicious "meatball" that pairs especially well with the nutty flavor of kamut-flour pasta. Use fresh beans or good-quality dried beans and many of your guests won't even recognize they aren't eating meat!

Cook the beans in boiling, salted water until tender, about 5 minutes. Once cool, use a spoon to press them through a mesh strainer to remove the skins and form a creamy paste. Mix the paste with the breadcrumbs, 3 tablespoons Parmesan, the egg, oregano, garlic powder, and salt and pepper to taste until combined. Wet your hands with water and roll 1-inch (2.5-cm) meatballs, adding more breadcrumbs or grated cheese if the mixture is too loose. You should get about a dozen meatballs.

Meanwhile, in a sauté pan large enough to hold the meatballs in one layer, heat 2 tablespoons oil and cook the onion until very soft. Add the tomato puree and salt and pepper to taste and simmer for 10 minutes. Finally, add in the meatballs, cover, and cook for 5 minutes without stirring, so as not to break apart the meatballs.

Boil the spaghetti in salted water until it is al dente. Drain and top with the sauce, meatballs, basil, and more grated Parmesan.

SPAGHETTI IN RED WINE

{ *Spaghetti al Nero d'Avola* }

SERVES 2* | REGION: *Sicily*

Instead of boiling the pasta in water until al dente, in this time-honored Sicilian recipe you will finish cooking it in red wine. The result is spaghetti with splendidly fruity tartness and lovely mahogany color. The trick to this dish is to add the wine only a few tablespoons at a time, so that it thickens into a glorious, deliciously fruity sweet glaze.

Chef Maurizio Botta, of Vecchia Cantina Baroni in Siracusa, adds a modern twist and serves it topped with ricotta, garnished with crisp frizzled leeks and sliced almonds for crunch.

In a bowl, mix the ricotta, 1 tablespoon oil, and salt, pepper, and nutmeg to taste until combined. Set aside.

Boil the spaghetti in salted water for just 3 minutes, then drain.

Meanwhile, in a sauté pan large enough to hold the pasta, fry half the leeks in 2 tablespoons oil on high heat until dark golden, about 4 minutes. Remove them with a slotted spoon and set them aside on paper towels.

Add the remaining leeks to the pan, lower the heat to medium, and cook until they are very soft, about 5 minutes. Add half the wine and the sugar and stir to combine. Toss in the parcooked spaghetti, raise the heat, and stir constantly, adding the remaining wine only a few tablespoons at a time. Toss the spaghetti frequently, keeping the heat high, so the wine is absorbed into the pasta. Cook until the pasta is al dente, adding more wine if needed. Stir in 2 tablespoons pecorino until it is fully incorporated, then taste and season with salt and pepper if needed.

Top each serving with a dollop of ricotta, some fried leeks, and a sprinkle of almonds.

¼ cup (60 g) ricotta, preferably sheep's milk

Olive oil

Salt and freshly ground black pepper

Freshly grated nutmeg

8 ounces (225 g) spaghetti

1 small leek, finely sliced

1 cup (240 ml) dry red wine, preferably Nero d'Avola, plus more if needed

2 teaspoons sugar

Grated pecorino cheese

Sliced almonds

If you'd like to serve four, double the ingredients and use two pans, because the sauce becomes velvety only when cooked in small batches.

ZUCCHINI-GLAZED PASTA

{ Pasta glassata }

SERVES 4 | **REGION:** *Throughout Italy*

It's a brilliant concept: Zucchini does double duty as both cooking medium and topping. After it's grated, it releases lots of delicious green juice, which is used to cook the pasta, coating it in a gorgeous glossy glaze. The grated pieces are then tossed with hot pasta to complete the light yet richly satisfying dish. Not a drop of vibrant, fresh vegetable flavor goes to waste.

This is one of my all-time favorite recipes—in fact, when PBS interviewed me for a special on Italian-Americans and asked about the pasta I most prefer, this is the one I mentioned. I love that it's light, healthy, and practically fat free; I love that it's simple but has a fancy, chef-y touch; I love how tasty and pretty it is. I love it!

6 large zucchini

Salt

2 garlic cloves, minced

1 pound (455 g) spaghetti or any long pasta

Olive oil

Parmesan or other aged cheese

Line a colander with cheesecloth and place it in a large bowl. Grate the zucchini on the smallest holes of a cheese grater into the colander. Toss the zucchini with a pinch of salt and the garlic and let it rest for 1 hour at room temperature.

Squeeze the zucchini to extract all the liquid; you should have about 1 cup of juice. Set aside both the grated zucchini and the juice.

Boil the pasta in lightly salted water for half the time suggested on the package, then drain it. In the empty pasta pot, bring the zucchini juice to a boil. Toss in the pasta and cook it, stirring occasionally, until it is al dente. Raise the heat to high at the end so any remaining juice absorbs into the pasta and creates a nice glaze.

Now you have a choice on how to finish the dish: You can either toss the pasta with the raw grated zucchini and top with a drizzle of olive oil or, if you prefer, fry the zucchini in a skillet on high heat with 2 tablespoons oil until crispy, then toss it into the pasta. Serve the pasta topped with grated or shaved cheese, if you like.

·5·

Fish

LECCARSI I BAFFI.

LICK YOUR MOUSTACHE.

Said of particularly delicious food.

Italians, with their long coastline, enjoy an abundant variety of seafood. In this chapter you'll find a wide assortment, including tuna, clams, mussels, eels and *baccalà*, paired with all sorts of unusual ingredients like creamy avocado and even licorice.

PURPLE PASTA

{ Linguine cotte all'estratto di cavolo rosso }

SERVES 2* | REGION: *Lombardy and northern Italy*

---

1 small head red cabbage, about
2 pounds (905 g)

8 ounces (225 g) linguine or any long
pasta, preferably Rummo brand

Salt

Olive oil

4 ounces (115 g) *burrata*, or
substitute fresh mozzarella plus 3
tablespoons heavy cream

3 ounces (90 g) smoked trout or
whitefish, flaked

¼ cup (35 g) toasted pistachio nuts

A few sprigs fresh watercress

**If you'd like to serve four, double
the ingredients and use two pans,
because the sauce becomes velvety
only when cooked in small batches.*

Pasta + Juicer = Dinner. In Italy today, many chefs—like the talented Andrea Aprea of Vun restaurant in Milan—are cooking pasta in vegetable extracts.

Here it's red cabbage juice, which produces pasta with a glorious purple color and lovely vegetal flavor. It's served with creamy *burrata* cheese for sweet richness, a touch of smoked fish for depth, pistachio nuts for crunch, and watercress for fresh brightness. It all makes a thrilling combination of vibrant colors, rich flavors, and varied textures.

Using an electric juicer, juice enough of the cabbage to get 1½ cups (360 ml) of liquid. In a skillet wide enough to hold the pasta, bring 1 cup (240 ml) of the juice to a boil.

Meanwhile, boil the pasta in a pot of salted water for 2 minutes. Drain and add to the cabbage juice to finish cooking, occasionally adding more juice a little at a time so it absorbs into the pasta and creates a glaze. When the pasta is al dente, stir in 1 to 2 tablespoons oil and toss over high heat for a few seconds until well combined.

Meanwhile, in a blender or small food processor, puree the cheese with a little oil until it is creamy.

Spread the cheese on the bottom of the serving plates, top with pasta, and garnish with the fish, pistachio nuts, and a few tiny watercress leaves.

TROUT & "SNAILS"

{ *Lumache alla Schegginese* }

SERVES 4 | REGION: *Umbria*

Olive oil

1 onion, minced

1 trout, about 1¾ pounds (800 g), gutted but with head and tail left on

Salt and freshly ground black pepper

1 cup (240 ml) dry white wine

1 (26-ounce/750-g) container strained tomatoes, preferably Pomi brand

1 cup vegetable or chicken broth

1 pound (455 g) *lumache* or any pasta

Black truffle, optional

Trout, caramelized onions, and tomatoes season the snails here . . . snail-shaped pasta, that is! With its big openings at both ends, *lumache* pasta lets lots of sauce sneak in.

The trout flavors the sauce and then is flaked to top the pasta. Then, traditionally, the pasta is topped with grated black truffles, which, along with trout, are specialties of the tiny hill town of Scheggino, where this recipe originates.

In a large pan over medium-high heat, warm ¼ cup (60 ml) oil and cook the onion until it is soft, about 5 minutes. Season the trout inside and out with salt and pepper and add it to the pan, pushing the onion to the side. Sear the trout on each side, remove it from the pan, and set aside.

Add the wine to the onions and bring it to a low boil. Stir in the tomatoes, return the trout to the pan, cover, and simmer over very low heat until the sauce thickens, about 1 hour, adding a little broth if needed. Remove the trout from the sauce. Flake the meat and reserve it to top the finished dish; discard the bones and skin.

Boil the pasta in salted water until it is al dente. Drain and toss into the sauce with a little of the cooking liquid. Add in a few tablespoons of shaved truffles, if using. Serve the pasta topped with more shaved truffles and the flaked trout.

TAGLIATELLE WITH SMOKED TROUT & LICORICE

{ *Tagliatelle al liquirizia con pesce affumicato* }

SERVES 4 | **REGION:** *Lombardy*

Smoked trout, fresh fava beans, creamy burrata cheese, and licorice: It's a startling list of ingredients that work in glorious, delicious harmony. The licorice leaves a fresh aftertaste, with a subtly piquant bite.

Sara Preceruti, at twenty-nine, is the youngest female chef in Italy to win a Michelin star, and she graciously taught me to make this dish. It has just the right balance of ingredients to complement the decisive intensity of the licorice. The result is an explosion of flavors with licorice as the final surprise.

The recipe calls for licorice pasta. You can buy it if it's available or try the great trick Chef Preceruti showed me—substitute any type of pasta and top the finished dish with ground licorice hard candies or a drizzle of licorice liqueur.

Combine the cream and cheese in the top of a double boiler or a buttered heatproof dish set over a pot of gently simmering water. Simmer on low, stirring every so often, for 10 minutes. Remove from the heat and blend with an immersion blender. Keep warm.

Meanwhile, boil the pasta in salted water until it is al dente.

In a nonstick frying pan large enough to hold the pasta, heat the garlic in 2 to 3 tablespoons oil until light golden, about 1 minute. Finely flake the trout and discard any skin and bones. Add the trout and wine to the pan, and simmer until the wine is reduced by half, about 5 minutes.

Cook the beans in boiling salted water for about 2 minutes, until they float to the surface and are tender. Peel the beans and add them to the trout sauce and stir until well combined. Toss the pasta into the sauce, adding a bit of cooking liquid if it is too dry.

Divide the warm burrata cream among the serving plates. Top with the pasta. If not using licorice pasta, sprinkle the top with finely crushed licorice candy or a drizzle of licorice liqueur.

½ cup (120 ml) heavy cream

4 ounces (115 g) burrata or fresh mozzarella cheese

1 pound (455 g) licorice-flavored tagliatelle, or any pasta plus Caffo's Liquorice liqueur or a few sugarless licorice hard candies (see Sources, page 200)

1 garlic clove, minced

Olive oil

4 ounces (115 g) smoked trout

¼ cup (60 ml) white wine

½ cup (60 g) fresh shelled fava beans

PASTA FROM A JAR

{ *Vasocottura* }

SERVES **2** *or* **4** *appetizer portions* | REGION: *Throughout Italy*

When Italians eat out of a jar, you can bet whatever's in there is homemade!

This is a great trick—cooking raw pasta in a Mason jar. It keeps all the aroma and flavors from escaping and makes for an adorable presentation. It's a modern technique, but based on the Italian tradition of oven-baked pasta.

Preheat the oven to 350°F (175°C).

In a large pan, heat 3 tablespoons oil over medium-high heat and add the onion and chile pepper to taste; cook until the onion is golden, about 8 minutes. Stir the lobster meat into the onions. Pour in the liqueur and bring everything to a low boil. Stir in the tomatoes, both broths, the pasta, garlic, basil leaves, and salt to taste.

Divide the mixture between pint- or quart-sized Mason jars, depending on how big a portion you'd like to serve, filling the jars no more than three fourths full to allow for the pasta to expand. Seal the jars closed. (Don't worry, they won't explode—Mason jars are thick and intended to be heated.) Stand the jars in a deep baking pan and add boiling water to the pan to reach halfway up the jars. Bake for about 25 minutes, then open one of the jars to test if the pasta is al dente. If not, return to the oven for another few minutes. Set the jars onto serving plates and serve them with grated cheese on the side.

Olive oil

1 large white onion, thinly sliced

1 small fresh red chile pepper, thinly sliced

1 small raw lobster tail, finely chopped

3 tablespoons wild fennel liqueur, or 3 tablespoons dry white wine plus ½ teaspoon crushed fennel seeds

1 (14-ounce/400-g) can diced tomatoes

1½ cups (360 ml) very hot vegetable broth

¾ cup (180 ml) very hot fish broth

8 ounces (225 g) *lumache* or other short pasta

2 garlic cloves, minced

12 large fresh basil leaves

Salt

Boiling water

Parmesan cheese

SEASIDE CARBONARA

{ Carbonara di mare }

SERVES 4 | REGION: *Throughout coastal Italy*

8 ounces (225 g) swordfish fillet

Salt and freshly ground black pepper

Olive oil

1 pound (455 g) linguine or other long pasta

4 large egg yolks

Grated pecorino cheese

2 garlic cloves, finely minced

Juice and zest of 1 lemon

Fresh parsley

There is perhaps no Italian dish more famous than carbonara: hot pasta tossed with raw egg yolks to create its own creamy sauce. This Italian beach favorite uses fish in place of the guanciale in traditional Roman carbonara. Here it's made with swordfish, but the silky lemony sauce makes a great base for virtually anything from the sea—grilled salmon, canned tuna, smoked trout, and even small raw clams.

Season the swordfish with salt and pepper. Put 1 tablespoon oil into a small sauté pan over high heat and sear the fish on both sides. Lower the heat and cook to the desired doneness, from rare to well done. Flake the fish into small pieces and set them aside.

Boil the pasta in salted water until it is al dente.

Meanwhile, in a large serving bowl, beat together the yolks, pepper, ¼ cup (25 g) of cheese, garlic, lemon juice, and half of the zest. Drain the pasta and toss into the bowl, stirring vigorously to heat the yolks to a creamy consistency. Stir in minced parsley to taste, a drizzle of oil, and the swordfish; season with salt and serve topped with the remaining zest.

STONE SOUP PASTA

The charming Massimo Riccioli, chef and owner of Rome's renowned seafood restaurant La Rosetta, told me about a dish he loved as a little boy: *pesce fuggito,* escaped fish. Pasta was boiled with sea stones as a stand-in for fish, especially during the poor years of the early 1950s. It was very popular along the coasts of Italy, especially in his region of Lazio.

"I was only a very little boy," recalls Massimo, "but I still remember how delicious, how fragrant that dish was—the stones from the sea added all the flavor that was needed and the sea water all the salt necessary to cook the pasta."

SPAGHETTI WITH SMOKY CLAM SAUCE & ROASTED TOMATOES

{ Spaghetti affumicati, vongole, e pendolini grigliati }

SERVES 4 | **REGION:** *le Marche*

Two–Michelin star chef Mauro Uliassi's updated version of Italy's iconic coastal dish—spaghetti with clam sauce—is a must-try. It's so good in fact that it was recently voted best dish of the year by *L'Espresso*, the prestigious guidebook to Italy's best restaurants!

Instead of cooking the clams in tomato sauce, the tomatoes are slow roasted to candylike sweetness and served on top. The pasta cooks only partway in boiling water, then finishes cooking in the smoked fish and clam sauce, to create a dish deeply infused with flavor.

Preheat the oven to 200°F (90°C). Line a baking sheet with parchment paper and lightly oil it.

Cut the tomatoes in half and arrange them, cut side up, on the prepared pan. Sprinkle them lightly with salt and the marjoram and thyme. Bake for 1½ hours, until they are shriveled and blackened at the edges. Set aside.

Simmer the broth and eel in a small saucepan for about 20 minutes to infuse the broth with smoky flavor. Strain the sauce and discard the eel. Set aside.

In another pot, bring 2 cups (480 ml) water to a boil. Add the clams, cover, and cook for about 10 seconds, until the shells open. Reserving the cooking liquid, remove the clams from their shells; set aside the meat and discard the shells.

In a large skillet, heat the garlic in 3 to 4 tablespoons oil until the garlic is golden. Add ½ cup (120 ml) of the eel broth and ½ cup (120 ml) of the clam cooking liquid.

Meanwhile, boil the pasta in lightly salted water for just 3 minutes. Drain the pasta and finish cooking it in the garlic-broth mixture over medium-high heat, stirring frequently, adding more broth until the pasta is al dente. Remove the pan from the heat and stir in the clams.

Serve the pasta topped with the roasted tomatoes, minced and whole parsley leaves, and pepper.

Olive oil

12 baby Roma, grape, or other small tomatoes

Salt

2 tablespoons fresh marjoram leaves

2 tablespoons fresh thyme leaves

1½ cups (360 ml) fish broth

8 ounces (225 g) smoked eel or trout

4 pounds (1.8 kg) very small clams, scrubbed

3 garlic cloves, sliced

1 pound (455 g) spaghetti or any long pasta

Fresh parsley

Freshly ground black pepper

TEENY TINY PASTA WITH CLAMS

{ *Fregula con arselle* }

SERVES 4 | **REGION:** *Sardinia*

---

2 pounds (910 g) very small clams, scrubbed

Olive oil

3 garlic cloves, minced

½ cup (120 ml) dry white wine

12 ounces (340 g) *fregula*, preferably Rustichella d'Abruzzo brand

5 oil-packed sundried tomatoes, thinly sliced

1 fresh red chile pepper, thinly sliced

Salt

Minced fresh parsley

Fregula, tiny toasted pasta nuggets from Sardinia, are like Israeli couscous but firmer, with a more toothsome bite. This is one of the classic *fregula* recipes. The sweet briny clams really show off the pasta's superb nutty flavor and extraordinary texture.

In a large saucepan, bring 1 quart (960 ml) water to boil. Add the clams, cover, and steam until they open, about 10 seconds. Remove almost all the clams from their shells, reserving a few in the shells for garnish. Strain the liquid through a fine-mesh sieve covered in cheesecloth to remove any sand, and reserve the liquid.

In a large skillet, heat 2 tablespoons oil and the garlic over medium heat until the garlic is light golden. Add the wine, fregula, tomatoes, and chile pepper to taste and simmer until most of the wine is absorbed, about 5 minutes. Add the clam liquid and boil, uncovered, stirring once or twice, until the fregola is al dente, 14 to 17 minutes or according to the package directions. It should not be too dry at the end, so if needed, add a little water or fish stock.

Season to taste with salt, stir in the cooked clams, and serve topped with parsley to taste, a drizzle of oil, and the reserved clams in their shells.

"WORMS" & EELS

{ Vermicelli con l'anguilla }

SERVES **4** | REGION: *Campania, Molise, Puglia, and other southern regions*

---

1 pound (455 g) eel, cleaned

Salt

Olive oil

1 bay leaf

1½ cups (360 ml) dry white wine

1 small onion, chopped

⅓ cup (30 g) minced fresh parsley

2 garlic cloves, crushed

1 small fresh red chile pepper, thinly sliced

1 (28-ounce/800-g) can diced tomatoes

1 pound (455 g) whole-wheat or farro vermicelli

The "worms" here are really ultra-thin vermicelli pasta, but the eels are real!

Eels have sweet, naturally smoky-tasting meat that's oh-so-tender—it's always the first piece I snag on any sushi platter. Eel goes especially well with whole-grain pasta, such as those made with nutty-tasting farro or kamut flour.

If you've never cooked with eel, this is a great first recipe to try. You can find eel in Asian fish markets or order it from your fishmonger. They will even gut and clean it for you and remove the head and tail. I've made this pasta dozens of times. When I have fussy eaters over to dinner, I don't mention that the sauce they're scarfing down—and raving about!—has eel. Since the meat is flaked, they can't tell, and think they're eating the world's best-tasting fish. I confess at dessert.

Rub the eel with salt to remove any viscous film on the skin, but do not peel off the skin itself. Rinse and cut the eel into bite-sized chunks.

In a large pan, heat 3 tablespoons oil and the bay leaf. Add the eel and cook over high heat until it is golden on both sides, then pour in ½ cup (120 ml) of the wine and scrape up any browned bits. Once the wine has burned off, remove the eel from the pan and set it aside.

Add the onion, half of the parsley, the garlic, and chile pepper to taste to the pan. When the onion is softened, add another ½ cup (120 ml) of the wine and cook on high until it is reduced by half. Stir in the tomatoes and simmer for 5 minutes, then add the remaining ½ cup (120 ml) of the wine and simmer until it is again reduced by half. Return the eel to the skillet and cook for 15 minutes, turning the pieces over now and then. Remove the eel from the sauce, peel off the skin, flake the meat, and discard the skin and bones. Return the meat to the sauce and season with salt.

Meanwhile, boil the pasta in salted water until it is al dente. Drain and toss into the sauce. Discard the bay leaf. Serve topped with remaining minced parsley.

BUCATINI WITH BACCALÀ & CRUNCHY WALNUTS

{ Sughetto di baccalà }

SERVES 4 | REGION: *Basilicata*

Dried codfish, *baccalà*—more intensely flavorful and with a firmer texture than fresh cod—pairs magnificently with pasta. I love the fantastic mix of savory and sweet in this recipe. The dense tomato sauce, rich with raisins, caramelized onion, tangy olives, and oregano, mingles well with the toothsome cod and crunchy walnuts.

Submerge the *baccalà* in a bowl of water, cover, and let soak in the refrigerator for 2 days, changing the water twice daily. Thinly slice or flake the *baccalà*, reserving ½ cup (120 ml) of the soaking liquid.

In a large skillet, combine ¼ cup (60 ml) oil and the onion and cook over medium-high heat until the onion is golden, about 5 minutes. Add the *baccalà*, the reserved ½ cup liquid, the tomato puree, olives, ⅓ cup (30 g) of minced parsley, raisins, oregano, and pepper to taste. Simmer on very low heat for 1 hour, until the flavors have fully melded.

Meanwhile, in a dry nonstick pan, re-toast the breadcrumbs until they are light golden. Drizzle with 2 tablespoons oil and add the walnuts. Cook, tossing often, until the crumbs are dark golden.

Boil the pasta in salted water until it is almost al dente. Drain and toss into the sauce with a little of the cooking liquid to finish cooking. Serve topped with the walnut breadcrumbs.

12 ounces (340 g) *baccalà*

Olive oil

1 large sweet onion, thinly sliced

1 (14-ounce/400-g) can tomato puree

14 pitted oil-cured black olives

Fresh parsley

¼ cup (40 g) raisins or currants

1 tablespoon dried oregano

Freshly ground black pepper

⅓ cup (37 g) homemade coarsely ground breadcrumbs, toasted

¼ cup (30 g) chopped walnuts

1 pound (455 g) *bucatini* or any pasta

NOTE: *Baccalà can sit in your pantry for months, but it does need to rehydrate in water for two days before you can cook with it.*

BLACK PASTA WITH MUSSELS

{ Pasta nera e frutta di mare }

SERVES 4 | REGION: *Calabria and southern Italy*

Squid ink pasta is hands-down one of the prettiest pastas ever! Glistening black, it's a glamorous canvas whose delicately briny flavor enhances any seafood. It is especially gorgeous against the lovely orange color of mussels.

In the photograph, the pasta is laid out straight, a style of plating popularized by Gualtiero Marchese, the Milan-born chef considered the founder of modern Italian cuisine. I've also seen modern Italian chefs arrange this pasta in a flat round spiral to look like the shiny black vinyl LPs of the past. Of course, you can serve it the conventional way too. It's delicious no matter how it's put on the plate!

In a large sauté pan over medium heat, cook the garlic in 3 tablespoons oil until it is aromatic. Add the mussels, tomatoes, beans, if using, and wine and cover. Cook until the mussel shells open, about 5 minutes, then remove almost all the mussels from their shells, reserving a few in the shell for garnish. Discard the shells and put the mussel meat back into the sauce.

To serve the pasta laid out straight, bring about 3 inches of salted water to a boil in two separate sauté pans, each wide enough to hold the pasta horizontally. Divide the pasta between the pans and boil until it is al dente. Using two tongs or a wide spatula, remove the pasta from the pans and, keeping it straight, lay it out onto a serving platter. (Alternatively, you can cook the pasta in a tall pot of boiling water and serve it in the conventional way.) Top with the sauce and reserved mussels in the shells. Season with salt and chile peppers. Serve topped with parsley.

3 garlic cloves, sliced

Olive oil

4 pounds (1.8 kg) mussels, scrubbed

1 (14-ounce/400-g) can diced tomatoes

½ cup (90 g) cooked small white beans like *cicerchie* or cannellini, optional

½ cup (60 ml) dry white wine

1 pound (455 g) squid ink pasta, preferably Felicetti or Rustichella d'Abruzzo brand

Salt

1 small fresh red chile pepper, thinly sliced, or red pepper flakes

Fresh parsley

SLOW-SIMMERED TUNA, CARAMELIZED ONIONS & "CANDLES"

{ Genovese di tonno }

SERVES 4 | **REGION:** *Campania, especially Naples*

Olive oil

2½ pounds (1.2 kg) yellow onions, sliced

1 celery stalk, minced

1 carrot, minced

2 cups (480 ml) dry white wine

1 cup (240 ml) vegetable or fish broth

1 pound (455 g) fresh tuna, cut into bite-sized cubes

Salt and freshly ground black pepper

1 pound (455 g) *candele*, cut into bite-sized pieces, or any thick tube pasta

A bushel of onions simmer slowly for hours creating caramel-sweetness that's accented with succulent, soft morsels of buttery tuna. This dish is traditionally served with *candele*, a long, thick candle-shaped pasta that's cut into pieces before cooking. But any thick pasta is perfect with this fantastic sauce.

Even people who think they don't like fish love this dish. The tuna transforms in the cooking process into something celestial.

In a large saucepan, heat ¼ cup (60 ml) oil over high heat. Cook the onions, celery, and carrots until they are caramelized, about 20 minutes. Add the wine, reduce the heat to low, cover, and simmer for 2 hours, stirring every half hour. Mix in the broth and tuna and cook, covered, for another hour, until the flavors have melded. Season with salt and pepper.

Boil the pasta in salted water until it is al dente. Drain and toss into the sauce, stirring until well combined. Serve hot, but note that it is generally not served topped with cheese or parsley.

PASTA WITH SPICY SNAIL SAUCE

{ Pasta al sugo di lumache }

SERVES 4 | REGION: *Abruzzo*

The French don't have a monopoly on escargots! Snails have been enjoyed in Italy since ancient Roman times, especially in southern Italy and Sicily. This recipe for snails in a spicy herb-infused tomato sauce comes from Abruzzo.

In a small sauté pan, heat 5 tablespoons olive oil and the garlic until the garlic is light golden. Add the snails, tomatoes, red pepper flakes to taste, and rosemary and simmer over very low heat for 10 minutes.

Meanwhile, boil the pasta in salted water until it is al dente. Drain and toss into the sauce; season to taste with salt. Serve sprinkled with the fresh herbs.

Olive oil

2 garlic cloves, minced

24 snails, either fresh or canned

6 fresh medium tomatoes, peeled, seeded, and chopped

Red pepper flakes

1 to 2 small sprigs fresh rosemary

Salt

1 pound (455 g) *spaghetti alla chitarra* or other long pasta

A few small leaves each of fresh parsley, mint, sage, and marjoram

LEMON-AVOCADO SPAGHETTI WITH SHRIMP

{ Spaghetti con avocado e gamberi }

SERVES 4 | **REGION:** *Sicily and southern Italy*

---

1 large red onion, finely sliced

¼ cup (60 ml) dry white wine

8 ounces (225 g) small shrimp, shelled and deveined

Olive oil

Salt

1 pound (455 g) spaghetti or any pasta, preferably Benedetto Cavalieri brand

1 avocado

Zest and juice of 1 lemon

Freshly ground black pepper

Avocados aren't indigenous to Italy, but as with tomatoes and corn, when these New World ingredients got there, the Italians did magical things with them.

Lemons and red onions, classic southern Italian ingredients, here combine with this creamy newcomer to the Mediterranean for an alluring fusion of textures and aromas. The avocado is used raw, and creates a healthier, more flavorsome "cream" in the sauce. The shrimp add briny tang and the lemon brightens the dish.

In a skillet large enough to hold the pasta, combine the onions and wine over medium heat and simmer until the onions are soft, about 10 minutes. Add the shrimp and raise the heat to high to evaporate any remaining wine; cook until the onions are caramelized and the shrimp are cooked, about 5 minutes. Off the heat, add 1 tablespoon oil and salt to taste.

Boil the pasta in salted water until it is al dente. Drain and toss with the onions.

Meanwhile, peel and pit the avocado and puree it with the lemon juice in a blender or small food processor until very smooth. Stir the mixture into the pasta and add half the lemon zest until well combined; re-season the dish with salt, if needed. Top the pasta with the remaining zest and pepper.

FISH HEADS, FISH HEADS

{ Mezzi rigatoni risottati con sugo scarti }

SERVES 4 | REGION: *Southern Italy*

Olive oil

1 onion, finely minced

1 small carrot, finely minced

1 celery stalk, finely minced

2 pounds (910 g) heads from monkfish or any large fish

1 cup (240 ml) dry white wine

1 garlic clove, minced

1 (26-ounce/750-g) container strained tomatoes, preferably Pomi brand

1 pound (455 g) mezzi rigatoni or other short tube pasta

Salt and freshly ground black pepper

A few fresh basil leaves

Quinto quarto

—

Fifth quarter

AN ITALIAN EXPRESSION *referring to dishes made up of the figurative fifth quarter of the animal, the usually discarded parts: organ meats, hooves, testicles, heads, and the like*

This sauce is made from fish heads, an underappreciated part of the fish that infuses the sauce with light, briny flavor. The pasta cooks right in the sauce, like risotto, permeating it with deep taste.

I like this dish so much, and make it so often, that my local fishmonger has taken to saving fish heads for me each week. I freeze them until I want to make another batch of pasta. *Grazie* to francesca D'Orazio Buonerba for teaching me this economical yet deliciously gourmet dish.

In a large saucepan, heat 2 tablespoons oil and cook the onion, carrot, and celery until they are soft, about 3 minutes. Add the fish heads and cook for a few minutes. Pour in the wine and scrape up any browned bits, then add 1 quart (960 ml) hot water. Bring to a boil, turn down the heat, and let simmer for 20 minutes. Strain the fish broth. If you like, pick through the heads for the tasty cheek meat to add to the broth; discard everything else. Keep the broth hot.

In another pot, large enough to hold the pasta, heat 2 tablespoons oil with the garlic, then add the tomatoes and bring them to a boil. Stir in the pasta, turn down the heat to medium-low, and simmer. Add the hot broth, a ladleful at a time, stirring occasionally, until the pasta is al dente and most of the sauce has been absorbed. If it is still too liquidy, raise the heat at the end to cook down some of the sauce. Season the pasta with salt and pepper and serve topped with torn basil leaves.

ZITI WITH OCTOPUS & ORANGE-ALMOND PESTO

{ Ziti al pesto di agrumi }

SERVES 4 | REGION: *Sicily and southern Italy*

Like summer on a fork! Oranges and almonds add delicate sweetness to this pesto, perfectly balanced with the zesty, salty tang of capers. It can be served with hot or room-temperature pasta, so it's great for buffets and picnics. In Sicily, they often top this fabulous citrus pesto with fish—like tuna, salmon, or shrimp—making a main-course dish. Here it's served with octopus, which you can boil or grill yourself or buy ready-cooked at a gourmet shop. It's even great with canned octopus, available at most supermarkets.

Finely grind the almonds in a small food processor, mortar and pestle, or clean coffee grinder. Add the basil and grind into a paste.

Using a very sharp knife, and working over a plate to collect the juices, cut off the skin and white pith of the oranges and discard. Separate the orange sections, cutting or peeling off the membranes between the sections. Add the orange sections, any collected orange juice, the capers, and 3 tablespoons oil to the almond mixture and grind into a paste, adding more oil if it is too thick. Season to taste with salt.

Boil the pasta in salted water until it is al dente. Drain and toss with the pesto. Serve hot or at room temperature, topped with cooked octopus.

²⁄₃ cup (100 g) blanched almonds

About 25 large fresh basil leaves

2 navel oranges

¹⁄₃ cup (45 g) salted capers, rinsed

Olive oil

Salt

1 pound (455 g) ziti or any pasta

12 ounces cooked octopus, sliced into bite-sized pieces

BEHIND THE SHAPE

Ziti, a pasta shape originating in southern Italy, gets its name from the dialect word for "bride and groom," *i zit*. There's another legend in Naples that claims this pasta got its name from the word *zite*, spinsters. Supposedly the women were single because of pasta! They'd stay home making pasta for the family's Sunday meal instead of attending church services and keeping on the lookout for a husband.

In Italy, ziti refers to short or long tube pasta, with the long sometimes called *zitone* and cooked either whole or cut into bite-sized pieces. Here in the States, we usually think of ziti in only the short version.

· 6 ·

Meat

This very popular Italian expression is said when mopping up sauce with a piece of bread, as it leaves an empty track in its wake. There's even a cute joke in Italian that references this saying: The prince offers Cinderella the glass slipper but she says, "No thanks, I'm full."

The saucy recipes in this chapter include a wide variety of meats, from duck, rabbit, and goat to beef and pork, and use them in every way possible, as Italians are apt to do, from the bones to the prime cuts. These hearty, satisfying dishes are guaranteed to have you *fare la scarpetta!*

3 MEATS, 2 SAUCES, 1 PASTA

{ *Sugo al ragù Piceno* }

SERVES **8** *to* **10** | REGION: *le Marche*

FOR THE FIRST SAUCE:

1 onion, quartered

6 whole cloves

Olive oil

2 pounds (910 g) mixed beef and pork bones

2 celery stalks, roughly chopped

1 carrot, roughly chopped

2 (26-ounce/750-g) containers strained tomatoes or *passata di pomodori*

1 bay leaf

Freshly grated nutmeg

Salt and freshly ground black pepper

FOR THE SECOND SAUCE:

1 celery stalk, very finely minced

1 small carrot, very finely minced

Olive oil

2 garlic cloves, very finely minced

1 sprig fresh rosemary

12 ounces (340 g) chicken livers and gizzards, finely minced

12 ounces (340 g) ground lean pork

12 ounces (340 g) ground lean beef

1 cup (240 ml) white wine

ingredient list continues

This dish is special because it's a combination of two sauces served at once. One is made with an assortment of bones simmered in tomatoes, then strained. The second sauce is a dense mix of minced beef, pork, and chicken, slow cooked in wine. The pasta is tossed with the first sauce, then plated and topped with the minced-meat sauce. The result is multiple levels of flavor.

It's generally served with *maccheroni di campofiglione*, special egg pasta that really absorbs the first sauce, making a rich base for the second sauce on top.

Here are two tips I learned in Italy for meat sauces: Stick whole cloves into a chunk of onion at the start of the sauce to infuse it with a hint of aromatic spice, and serve the pasta accompanied by a small plate holding scissors and whole dried chile peppers so everyone can add a pinch of heat.

Make the first sauce: Stud the onion quarters with the cloves. In a large saucepan, heat ¼ cup (60 ml) oil over medium heat. Add the onions, bones, celery, and carrot and sauté until the vegetables are very soft, about 30 minutes. Add the tomatoes, bay leaf, and nutmeg to taste and bring them to a boil. Reduce the heat and simmer, covered, for at least 3 hours. The sauce should not be thick, more like stock, so add a little water if needed. Strain the sauce, discarding the bones and vegetables. Season to taste with salt and pepper.

Make the second sauce: In a medium saucepan, combine the celery, carrot, 5 tablespoons oil, the garlic, and rosemary and cook over medium-high heat until soft, about 5 minutes. Add the chicken liver and gizzards and cook just 1 minute, until they are no longer red inside. Stir in the pork and beef, breaking up any large pieces with a wooden spoon, and cook until browned. Add the wine, turn down the heat to low, and simmer for about 30 minutes, until the flavors have melded. Add 1 cup of the first sauce to the pot, and simmer for another 5 minutes. Season to taste with salt and pepper.

recipe continues

2 pounds (910 g) thin egg pasta such as *maccheroni di campofiglione,* preferably Spinosi brand

Parmesan cheese

Dried whole chile peppers

To serve: Boil the pasta in salted water until it is al dente. Drain and toss with the first sauce until the sauce is well absorbed. Using a large fork, twirl portions onto the serving plates. Top each portion with a ladleful or two of the second sauce and sprinkle it with grated cheese. Accompany the pasta with a plate of dried chile peppers and small scissors so guests can help themselves.

UNDISCOVERED ITALY: ASCOLI PICENO

I first tasted this dish in the charming medieval town of Offida, in the Ascoli Piceno province of the le Marche region, at the restaurant Cantina del Picchio. I left so impressed with this jewel of a province and its fabulous foods and wines that I decided to feature Ascoli Piceno in a series of talks I give in New York called "Undiscovered Italy." The president of the province got wind of the upcoming talks and arranged for the restaurant's chef, Mr. Pasqualini, to come to New York to cook for the various audiences I'd be addressing. In addition to teaching me the nuances of this stand-out dish, he wowed the audience at each event with his delicious creation!

"GUITARS" & RABBITS

{ *Ragù di coniglio e vino bianco* }

SERVES 6 | **REGION:** *Abruzzo*

Rabbit, slow-roasted until buttery and melting off the bone, is the base of this outstanding sauce, created by two–Michelin star chef Niko Romito. "Guitars" refers to the four-sided *pasta alla chitarra* shape that is traditionally served with this dish, which is made on a stringed pasta cutter called a *chitarra*.

You'll love the delicate touch of lemon zest and the full, rich flavor produced by the slow cooking. Plus, the sauce only takes a few minutes of hands-on preparation, as most of the work is done in the oven.

Preheat the oven to 200°F (90°C).

Put the carrot, onion, celery, and garlic into a Dutch oven or ovenproof pot on the stove with 3 to 4 tablespoons oil. Cook for about 20 minutes on medium heat, until the vegetables are soft.

Add the rabbit, raise the heat to high, and sear the meat on all sides. Pour in the wine, scraping up any brown bits with a wooden spoon. Add the thyme, rosemary, and marjoram and season with salt. Using a vegetable peeler, peel off only the yellow zest of the lemon in large sections and stir them into the pot. Place aluminum foil close to the surface of the meat, then cover the pot with a lid and put it into a roasting pan half filled with hot water. Bake for 4 hours, stirring occasionally.

Remove the rabbit from the pan and discard the bones and skin. Pass the vegetables and pan juices through a strainer. Put the pan juices and the meat back into the pan and keep warm; discard the vegetable solids.

Boil the pasta in salted water until it is al dente. Drain the pasta, toss it into the sauce, and serve it topped with grated cheese.

1 carrot, roughly chopped

1 onion, roughly chopped

1 celery stalk, roughly chopped

1 garlic clove, roughly chopped

Olive oil

One (2½- to 3-pound/1.2- to 1.4-kg) rabbit, cut into 6 pieces

2 cups (480 ml) dry white wine, preferably Trebbiano d'Abruzzo

A few sprigs each fresh thyme, rosemary, and marjoram

Salt

1 lemon

1 pound (455 g) *spaghetti alla chitarra* or other long pasta, preferably Rustichella d'Abruzzo brand

Parmesan cheese

LEEK-GLAZED SPAGHETTINI WITH PANCETTA

{ *Spaghettini glassate ai porri* }

SERVES 2* | **REGION:** *Abruzzo*

---

4 pounds (1.8 kg) leeks

2 ounces (60 g) pancetta or bacon, finely minced

½ cup (120 ml) white wine

Salt

Cayenne

8 ounces (225 g) spaghettini, vermicelli, or other thin pasta, preferably Verrigni brand

Olive oil

Parmesan cheese

*If you'd like to serve four, double the ingredients and use two pans, because the sauce becomes velvety only when cooked in small batches.

Flame-charred leeks are juiced and then combined with bits of smoky pancetta and a touch of wine. The pasta cooks right in these delicious liquids, creating a silky, glossy sauce. An outstanding dish!

This masterpiece is by Michelin-star chef Niko Romito, who introduced me to Verrigni pasta, made by pressing the dough through solid gold extruders. For this dish he uses their "super spaghettini," well worth searching out, as it is exceptionally thin yet with a nice toothsome consistency. Of course, you can substitute any good-quality, long, thin pasta, like angel hair.

Preheat the broiler or a grill to medium-high heat.

Wash the leeks and cut off the root ends, but keep the leeks whole. Broil or grill them until the outer leaves are charred and the insides soft, turning to char all sides, 30 to 40 minutes. Once they are cool, process the leeks through a juicer or vegetable extruder. Discard the pulp; reserve the juice.

In a skillet wide enough to hold the raw pasta horizontally, cook the pancetta over medium heat until crisp, about 3 minutes. Pour in the wine, scraping up any brown bits with a wooden spoon. Add ¼ cup (60 ml) of the leek juice, season with salt and a pinch of cayenne, and bring to a boil. Add the pasta and stir, adding additional leek juice a few ladlefuls at a time as needed, until the pasta is al dente, about 6 minutes. At the end, stir in 1 or 2 tablespoons oil and toss over high heat until all the leek juice is absorbed and the pasta has a pretty glaze.

Twirl forkfuls of pasta onto a plate and serve immediately. Sprinkle on finely grated cheese, ideally grated on a Microplane.

PASTA FIT FOR A KING

{ *Maccheroni con le rigaglie* }

SERVES 4 | **REGION:** *Lazio, especially the Romano-Castellana areas, but also popular in the Veneto*

Full disclosure: *rigaglie*, a word that comes from the Latin for "royal gift," in fact means "chicken giblets" in Italian. The sauce, even though it is made of poultry parts often discarded, is actually a delicacy, very refined and with deep, rich flavor. Be brave and add cockscombs, too! They not only have a nice texture and lovely flavor, but are very pretty on the plate.

I love the tip I learned in Italy about infusing the cooking wine with herbs and garlic for an hour before cooking with it—a trick that adds lots of extra flavor to any recipe!

Combine the wine, 2 sprigs marjoram, and the garlic in a cup and let them infuse for 1 hour.

Mince the giblets, but leave the cockscomb whole, if using. In a large skillet, heat 3 tablespoons oil over high heat. Add the giblets and cockscomb and cook until they are browned, about 2 minutes. Pour in the wine, garlic, and marjoram and scrape up any brown bits with a wooden spoon. Stir in the tomatoes (or if using tomato paste, mix with 1 cup water until smooth, then stir in), reduce the heat to very low, and simmer until the sauce thickens, about 1½ hours. Season with salt and pepper, and remove the garlic and herb sprigs.

Boil the pasta in salted water 1 minute shy of al dente. Drain and toss into the sauce to finish cooking, adding a few tablespoons of cooking liquid. Serve the pasta topped with grated cheese, sprigs of marjoram, and diced tomato.

½ cup (120 ml) red wine

Several sprigs fresh marjoram

1 garlic clove, crushed

Olive oil

1 pound (455 g) assorted chicken giblets such as gizzards, liver, heart, and cockscomb

1 cup (250 g) strained tomatoes or *passata di pomodori,* or 3 tablespoons tomato paste

Salt and freshly ground black pepper

1 pound (455 g) *spaghettoni* or other long pasta, preferably Benedetto Cavalieri brand

Aged pecorino cheese

1 tomato, diced

DUCK VENETIAN STYLE WITH BIGOLI

{ Bigoli co' l'arna }

SERVES 4 | REGION: *Veneto*

2 to 3 shallots, roughly chopped

1 celery stalk, roughly chopped

2 garlic cloves

Olive oil

5 fresh sage leaves

1 bay leaf

3 sprigs fresh thyme

1 boneless duck breast, without skin, ground (about 1 pound)

1 cup duck stock

1 pound *bigoli* or other long, thick pasta

Vezzena, Parmesan, or other aged cheese, grated

Arna lessa e bigolo tondo, a la sera i contenta el mondo.

—

Boiled duck and round bigoli at dinner and all's right with the world.

—VENETIAN PROVERB

Bigoli are a long, thick pasta specialty of the Veneto. In the past, this dish was made by cooking the pasta in broth made from a whole duck, then topping it with the duck giblets sautéed in butter and sage. But even Venetian grannies don't make it that way anymore. Nowadays, this lighter version, still very luscious and rich, uses just one duck breast instead of the entire bird—you can ask your butcher to grind it for you, or do it yourself by rough chopping it or putting it through the meat grinder attachment on your food processor.

In a small food processor or a mortar and pestle, grind the shallots, celery, and garlic. In a large skillet, heat 3 tablespoons oil over medium-high heat. Add the shallot mixture, sage, bay leaf, and thyme and cook until softened. Add the duck and sauté until browned, about 4 minutes. Add the stock, cover, and simmer on low for 1 hour, until the flavors have melded and the sauce is thick. Remove the bay leaf and thyme.

Boil the pasta in salted water until it is al dente. Drain and toss into the sauce along with a few tablespoons of the cooking liquid. Stir for several minutes in the skillet to combine the flavors. Serve the pasta topped with grated cheese.

BEHIND THE SHAPE

Bigoli are traditionally made by passing the dough through a special device called a *torchio*, but nowadays they're often made with just a regular pasta extruder or the large holes in a home meat grinder attachment. In the Veneto region, *bigoli* are often made with duck eggs, which act as a wonderful binder for the flour.

ONIONY NEAPOLITAN MEAT SAUCE WITH CANDELE

{ Pasta alla Genovese }

SERVES 8 to 10 | REGION: *Campania, especially Naples*

This is a dish you'll eat midday on Sunday at a friend's home in Naples, with its succulent aromas greeting you down the block.

The sauce requires lots of onions, so employ whatever tricks you must to prevent tears—just don't skimp on the onions! When in doubt, add more onions, never less. The onions slow cook with the meat until they take on a dark, caramel-like depth of flavor and silky creaminess. *Slow cooked* is the key phrase here, because when Italians say "slow," they mean it—four to five hours slow. You'll be rewarded with a good-down-to-your-toes sauce that lovingly clings to the pasta.

In the bottom of a large saucepot, heat 3 to 4 tablespoons oil over medium heat. Add the lard, if using, and the beef. Brown the beef on all sides. Do not salt the meat yet. Once the meat has browned on all sides, pour in 1½ cups (360 ml) of the wine, scraping up any brown bits on the bottom of the pot. Cook until the wine completely evaporates, then stir in the onions, celery, and carrots. Put a piece of aluminum foil directly on top of the onions, then cover the pot with a lid. Reduce the heat to very low and cook for 3 hours, until the meat is fork tender. Remove the meat to a serving platter and cover. Add the remaining ½ cup (120 ml) wine to the sauce and continue to cook the sauce for another hour, until the onions are very soft and the mixture is thick and dark golden.

When you are ready to serve, boil the pasta in salted water until it is al dente. Drain and toss in a large serving bowl with the onion sauce, mixing in lots of grated cheese. If you like, you can add in a little of the meat, shredded into small pieces, or serve the meat as a second course. Serve the pasta with grated cheese and a peppermill on the side, so guests can add to taste.

Olive oil

1 heaping tablespoon lard, optional

3 pounds (1.4 kg) beef chuck or shoulder, cut into 4 chunks

About 2 cups (480 ml) dry white wine

6½ pounds (3 kg) yellow onions, thinly sliced

2 celery stalks, very finely minced

1 large carrot, very finely minced

2 pounds (910 g) *candele*, broken into pieces, or any thick pasta, preferably Garofalo brand

Salt

Parmesan cheese

Freshly ground black pepper

BY ANY OTHER NAME

This sauce is called *alla Genovese*, but despite its name it is not from Genoa. There's lots of debate in Naples as to the name's origin. According to the two most popular legends, either it was first cooked in Naples, but by a chef from Genoa, or the chef's last name was actually "Genovese."

MEAT & PEAR OPEN RAVIOLI

{ *Casconcelli aperti alla Bergamasca* }

SERVES 4 | **REGION:** *Lombardy, especially Bergamo*

The concept of using ravioli filling as a condiment for pasta is very liberating! Open ravioli was popularized by the famous Italian chef Gualtiero Marchesi, who first introduced *ravioli aperti* back in the 1980s. Nowadays, many Italians, pressed for time, forgo ravioli making and turn the filling into a free-form sauce for pasta. The flavors are the same and it saves time.

Bergamo, in Lombardy, is renowned for its *casconcelli*—highly delicious, very unusual ravioli made with an odd but oh-so-tasty assortment of ingredients: salami, roast beef, pears, raisins, and crushed almond cookies.

In a large skillet, melt the butter over medium-high heat. Add the pancetta and cook until it is crisp, about 5 minutes. Remove the sausage from the casing and crumble it into the pan; cook until browned. Add the beef, pear, raisins, garlic, and sage. Cook the mixture until the pears are soft.

Meanwhile, boil the pasta in salted water until it is almost al dente. Drain and toss into the sauce along with a few tablespoons of the cooking liquid. Stir well and cook, adding more cooking liquid if needed, until the pasta is al dente. Stir in the zest and season with grated cheese, cinnamon, nutmeg, and parsley to taste. Season with salt and pepper and serve the pasta topped with a sprinkling of amaretti crumbs.

3 tablespoons butter

2 ounces (60 g) pancetta or bacon, diced

1 sweet sausage

4 ounces (115 g) roast beef, thinly sliced, then cut into strips

1 large pear, thinly sliced, with peel left on

2 tablespoons golden raisins

1 garlic clove, minced

3 to 4 small fresh sage leaves

1 pound (455 g) *calamarata* or other tube pasta

Zest of ½ lemon

Grana padano or other aged cheese

Ground cinnamon

Freshly grated nutmeg

Minced fresh parsley

Salt and freshly ground black pepper

2 or 3 amaretti cookies, crushed

CAVATELLI WITH GOAT RAGÙ

{ Cavatelli al sugo di capra }

SERVES 4 | **REGION:** *Campania, especially the province of Salerno*

---

2 pounds (910 g) goat leg meat, cut into 5 slices

About 1 cup (115 g) grated aged pecorino cheese

⅓ cup (30 g) minced fresh parsley

5 garlic cloves, minced

Salt and freshly ground black pepper

Olive oil

1 onion, minced

1 cup (240 ml) dry white wine

1 (26-ounce/750-g) container strained tomatoes or *passata di pomodori*, preferably Pomi or Alice Nero brands

1 pound (455 g) *cavatelli* or other short pasta

Goat cheese, goat yogurt, and even goat's milk are available in most supermarkets and are increasingly common in the States. It's time for us Americans to appreciate the rest of the goat! Goat is the world's most widely consumed red meat, and it's especially popular in southern Italy.

Rolled slices of succulent goat meat, filled with cheese, garlic, and parsley, are braised here in tomatoes. Because it slow cooks for hours, the resulting sauce gets deeply infused with flavor. The pasta is tossed with the sauce and then served with thin slices of the tender rolled meat.

Using a meat mallet or the bottom of a cast-iron skillet, pound the meat slices until as thin as possible. Sprinkle them with the cheese, parsley, garlic, and salt and pepper to taste. Tightly roll up each slice and tie it with kitchen twine.

In a large sauté pan, heat 2 tablespoons oil over medium-high heat. Add the onion and cook until it is golden, about 12 minutes. Push the onion to the side of the pan and add the goat rolls. Brown each roll on all sides, adding a little more oil if needed. Pour in the wine, stir the onion and rolls together, and simmer until the wine completely evaporates. Add the tomatoes, cover, and simmer on low for 2 hours, turning the rolls occasionally, until very tender. Season the sauce to taste with salt and pepper.

Boil the pasta in salted water until it is al dente. While the pasta is cooking, remove the goat rolls from the pot. Thinly slice one or two of the rolls. (The rest of the rolls, topped with a little sauce and grated cheese, can be served on a platter on the side or as a second course.) Drain the pasta, toss it into the sauce, and mix well. Serve it topped with a couple slices of the meat and shaved or grated cheese, if you like.

BEHIND THE SHAPE

Cavatelli, a specialty of southern Italy, are made by rolling walnut-sized sections of pasta dough across a wooden board with a finger or blunt knife, making a little indentation. In Italy, there's a special tool for this called *sferre*. The name of the pasta comes from *cavato*, to carve out. They are available in the States fresh or dried.

CRUNCHY-TENDER PASTA SQUARES

{ *Basotti* }

SERVES 4 | **REGION:** *Romagna section of Emilia-Romagna*

This is a contrast in textures—crunchy outside with a soft cheesy center. *Basotti* is a hallmark dish of *cucina familiare*, or home cooking, that is virtually unknown even in Italy, outside of Romagna.

To understand the importance of this traditional recipe, you need to go back sixty to seventy years, when the economic conditions of Emilia-Romagna were dire. This dish was once made with whatever was on hand, such as leftover pasta baked at the side of the hearth in a bit of broth, topped with a slice of lardo, if the farmer was lucky enough to have any. Nowadays they can splurge and put butter and grated cheese on top!

This recipe is simple to assemble, but must be made with egg pasta, either fresh or dried. You don't need much pasta, as egg pasta expands as it bakes and absorbs the cheese and broth. Speaking of broth, since it provides most of the flavor, it's best to use homemade.

10 tablespoons (140 g) butter, thinly sliced

2 tablespoons breadcrumbs, toasted

8 ounces (225 g) egg *tagliolini* or another very thin egg noodle, preferably Spinosi brand

About 2 cups (230 g) grated Parmesan cheese

Freshly grated nutmeg

1 quart (960 ml) very hot pork, beef, or chicken broth

Preheat the oven to 400°F (205°C). Generously butter an 8-by-15-inch (20-by-38-cm) metal baking pan and sprinkle it with the breadcrumbs.

Layer half of the pasta in the pan and top it with half of the sliced butter, a third of the cheese, and 1 tablespoon nutmeg. Add the remaining pasta in a thin scattered layer on top. Top it with the remaining butter and more nutmeg.

Ladle the broth over the pasta until the noodles are just covered. Sprinkle the top with half of the remaining cheese. Bake for 35 to 40 minutes, until the pasta is firm to the touch.

Raise the oven temperature to 475°F (245°C).

Top the pasta with the remaining cheese and bake for a few minutes more, until it is crispy on top. Cut the basotti into squares and serve it hot.

Savory Chocolate & Coffee

CON LE TRE C.

WITH THREE Cs.

What Neapolitans say when ordering coffee. The "Cs" refer to comm cazz coce,
which features men's anatomy . . . politely translated as "very hot."

This unusual savory chapter includes recipes that feature either coffee or chocolate.

As you might expect from the nation that invented the espresso machine and is renowned for its fabulous roasting techniques, Italians perform magic in the kitchen with coffee. Italians add coffee to pasta sauce, mix it right into pasta dough itself, or simply add a dusting to the finished plate. Coffee adds a complex richness to savory dishes, with hints of roasted nuts and pleasing bitterness.

Chocolate is an equally marvelous ingredient with pasta. Like wine, fine dark chocolate has an amazingly complex taste profile, with hundreds of distinct nuanced aromas and flavors.

When cacao beans arrived in Italy in the sixteenth century, the Italians quickly realized that, despite the name, cacao beans are seeds, not beans. And just like many seeds—fennel, cardamom, caraway—cacao beans are a spice. It's only the addition of sugar that makes chocolate a sweet. So the Italians ground and toasted the cacao beans and used them in many savory dishes.

INSTANT CHOCOLATE PASTA WITH ORANGE-BASIL CREAM

{ *Garganelli al cioccolato in salsa di mascarpone* }

SERVES 4 | REGION: *Throughout northern and central Italy*

Salt

12 ounces (340 g) *garganelli* or any pasta, preferably Rustichella d'Abruzzo brand

⅓ cup (30 g) unsweetened cocoa powder

⅓ cup (40 g) finely chopped hazelnuts

2 tablespoons butter

⅓ cup (75 ml) Grand Marnier or other orange liqueur

¾ cup (180 ml) heavy cream

4 ounces (120 g) mascarpone cheese

Grated Parmesan or *grana padano* cheese

A few small fresh basil leaves

Dark chocolate

Milk chocolate

Zest of 1 orange, cut into long strips

I'm crazy about this Italian trick of adding a little cocoa powder to the water when boiling pasta. It makes instant chocolate pasta, rich and earthy. Delicious, nuanced, and surprisingly savory—the chocolate pasta is combined with creamy mascarpone infused with hints of orange liqueur, fragrant basil, and crunchy hazelnuts. It's simple to make, yet tastes special-occasion gourmet!

Bring a pot of salted water to a boil. Add the pasta and cocoa and boil until the pasta is al dente.

Meanwhile, in a sauté pan large enough to later toss the pasta, toast the hazelnuts in the butter over medium heat until aromatic, about 5 minutes. Pour in the Grand Marnier and stir a few seconds to burn off the alcohol. Reduce the heat to low, add the cream and mascarpone and stir until creamy.

Drain the pasta and toss it with the sauce. Add cheese and salt to taste. Serve topped with the basil, grated dark and milk chocolates to taste, and the zest.

BEHIND THE SHAPE

The pasta shape pictured here is *garganelli*, chicken gullet, named for its distinctive ridges that look like the wrinkles on a chicken's neck. They are made fresh using small squares of dough rolled onto a thin rod and then pressed against a special comblike device called a *pettine*. They are also available commercially made and dried. One of my favorite tall tales about this pasta's creation is a sort of "dog ate my homework" story. According to legend, the cat ate the filling for the tortellini a poor farmer's wife was making for guests about to arrive. Since she had already cut the dough squares for the tortellini she decided to pretty them up by rolling them and pressing them closed against the strings on her loom.

MAFALDE WITH MUSSELS IN VELVETY CHOCOLATE SAUCE

{ *Vellutata di cozze e cioccolata* }

SERVES 2* | **REGION:** *Campania, especially Ischia*

1½ pounds (680 g) mussels, scrubbed and beards removed

1 thin zucchini, very thinly sliced

Olive oil

1 garlic clove, minced

Red pepper flakes

½ cup (120 ml) dry white wine

1 teaspoon tomato paste

1 tablespoon fresh mozzarella *di bufala* or heavy cream

1 ounce (30 g) milk chocolate, chopped, preferably Perugina brand

8 ounces (225 g) *mafalde, lasagnotte,* or other wide, flat pasta, cut into bite-sized pieces

Grated Parmesan cheese

A few fresh parsley leaves

*If you'd like to serve four, double the ingredients and use two pans, because the sauce becomes velvety only when cooked in small batches.

Mussels in a satiny, rich sauce: If you don't tell them, your friends will never guess that the secret to the special flavor is chocolate! Like wine, vinegar, and lemon juice, chocolate provides just the right touch of acidity; it also acts as an emulsifier, adding natural thickness to the sauce.

The province of Naples has been an important center for chocolate production in Italy for centuries, so it's logical that they'd cook with chocolate. What is less obvious is that they'd cook *seafood* with chocolate! The touch of milk chocolate leaves a lingering hint of creaminess. I thought it would be too weird for words, but this pairs superbly with the mussels' natural briny sweetness.

Put the mussels in a skillet large enough to later toss the pasta. Sprinkle them with a few tablespoons water, cover, and bring to a boil until the shells open, about 5 minutes. Remove the mussels from the shells, put the meat into a bowl along with any pan liquids, and set aside. Discard the shells.

In the same pan, heat 2 tablespoons oil over high heat. Add the zucchini and fry until it is golden. Stir in the garlic, red pepper flakes to taste, and the reserved mussels and simmer for 1 minute, stirring to combine. Add the wine and raise the heat for a few minutes to evaporate the alcohol. Add the tomato paste and 2 tablespoons water, stir to combine, then lower the heat; simmer the mixture for an additional 5 minutes, then take it off the heat. Add the mozzarella and chocolate and stir until both dissolve.

Meanwhile, boil the pasta in salted water for 4 minutes less than the package directs. Drain and toss into the sauce. Cook it all over low heat, adding a bit of the liquid from the mussels, if needed, until the pasta is al dente. Remove it from the heat, and add Parmesan to taste, stirring until it is melted. Divide the pasta between two plates, and garnish with parsley.

PORK RAGÙ WITH HINTS OF CHOCOLATE

{ *Sciabbó* }

SERVES 4 | REGION: *Sicily, the province of Enna*

This specialty of Enna, a province in Sicily, is served in the winter, especially during the Christmas holidays. The touches of chocolate and cinnamon add aroma and richness and the dash of dessert wine imparts a deep mellow sweetness to this remarkable ragù.

This dish, which dates to the 1700s, is traditionally made with pretty curly-edged noodles called *lasagne ricce*, which look like the ruffles that were popular on men's shirts back then. The name of the dish, *sciabbó*, is in fact a Sicilian corruption of *jabot*, the French word for those shirts.

In a large saucepan, heat 2 tablespoons oil over medium-high heat. Add the onion and sauté until it is soft, about 12 minutes. Add the pork and cook until it is browned, about 5 more minutes. Add the wine, turn down the heat to medium-low, and simmer for several minutes to burn off the alcohol. Stir in the tomato puree, cinnamon, chocolate, and sugar to taste. Season with salt and pepper, cover, and simmer for 1 hour, stirring occasionally, until the pork is tender. Remove the cinnamon stick.

Boil the pasta in salted water until it is al dente. Drain and toss into the sauce until well combined. This pasta is not traditionally topped with grated cheese.

Olive oil

1 large yellow onion, minced

8 ounces (225 g) lean pork loin, finely diced

½ cup (120 ml) dessert wine like vin santo or Marsala

1 (28-ounce/800-g) can tomato puree

1 (2-inch/5-cm) cinnamon stick

2 ounces (60 g) dark chocolate, chopped, preferably Perugina brand

1 to 2 tablespoons sugar

Salt and freshly ground black pepper

1 pound (455 g) *lasagne ricce*, *lasagnotte*, or any thick ribbon pasta

SAVORY CHOCOLATE

Recipes for savory dishes with chocolate were published in Italy as far back as 1680 and included lasagne in anchovy-almond-chocolate sauce; pappardelle in rabbit-chocolate sauce; fried liver accented with dark chocolate; and polenta topped with chocolate, breadcrumbs, almonds, and cinnamon. It was such common practice to season foods with chocolate that Francesco Arisi, in his 1736 poem "Il Cioccolato," pokes fun at chefs who overuse it.

SPAGHETTI WITH ROSEMARY & CACAO NIBS

{ Spaghetti con fiori di rosmarino e fave di cacao }

SERVES 4 | REGION: *Northern and central Italy*

---

1 pound (455 g) spaghetti or any long pasta

Salt

8 tablespoons (115 g) butter

3 tablespoons fresh rosemary leaves, plus flowers if available

Grated Parmesan cheese

Freshly ground black pepper

3 tablespoons cacao nibs

This stunning, aromatic dish is so simple you barely need a recipe. Spaghetti tossed with a bit of butter, Parmesan cheese, and rosemary is topped with cacao nibs. Nibs, little broken-up bits of toasted cacao beans, are chocolate in its purest state: no sugar or other flavorings, just fabulous 100 percent chocolate with a pleasing bitterness and nutty rich taste.

Dubious about the combo? Do a quick taste-test. Put a pinch of Parmesan in the palm of your hand. Add a few cacao nibs and a tiny bit of fresh rosemary. Pop it all into your mouth and chew . . . see what I mean? Now, hurry—go start the water boiling!

Boil the spaghetti in salted water for 2 minutes less than package directs. Drain, reserving some of the cooking liquid, and return the pasta to the pot. Stir in the butter, half of the rosemary and flowers, and Parmesan to taste. Toss until the butter melts, adding a little cooking liquid until the sauce is creamy.

Serve the pasta topped with pepper, a sprinkle of cacao nibs, and the remaining rosemary.

SPAGHETTI WITH ONIONS, ANISE & ESPRESSO

{ Spaghetti con crema di cipolle, anice stellato, e caffé }

MAKES *4 appetizer portions* | **REGION:** *Veneto*

Espresso with a shot of anise-flavored Sambuca liqueur is a classic Italian flavor combination. But star anise and coffee with pasta?

Surprising as it sounds, three–Michelin star chef Massimiliano Alajmo makes the combination work amazingly well. It's elegantly simple, with caramelized onions pureed with Parmesan to create a savory-sweet sauce that is drizzled with espresso–star anise syrup to add a mouthwatering licorice-like aroma and nutty roasted richness. It's especially delicious served with hearty whole-grain farro pasta. As the flavors are fairly intense, this is best served in small portions as the starter course.

In a very small saucepan, combine the star anise, a pinch of salt, and ½ cup (120 ml) cold water. Simmer over very low heat until the liquid is reduced by half, about 10 minutes. Off the heat, stir in the sugar and cornstarch until dissolved. Tilting the saucepan (there isn't much liquid so it needs to be concentrated in one spot), return it to the heat and simmer until the remaining liquid is thick, about 30 seconds. Remove it from the heat and stir in the espresso until well combined. Transfer everything to an espresso cup or other small container, cover with plastic wrap, and reserve.

In a skillet, heat 2 tablespoons oil over very low heat. Add the onions and sauté until they are very soft, about 15 minutes. Using a small food processor or an immersion blender, puree the onions with an additional 2 to 3 tablespoons oil, and salt and pepper to taste.

Meanwhile, boil the pasta in salted water until it is al dente.

Spread 1 tablespoon of the onion puree onto the center of each serving plate. Drain the pasta and toss it with the rest of the puree and ¼ cup (30 g) of Parmesan. With a large fork, twirl a portion of pasta into a nest shape on each plate, top with the remaining onion mixture, and drizzle the syrup on the pasta and around the plate. Garnish each plate with a star anise from the syrup.

4 whole star anise

Salt

1 teaspoon sugar

½ teaspoon cornstarch

1 shot, about 2 ounces (60 ml), freshly brewed espresso

8 ounces (225 g) farro or whole-wheat spaghetti

Olive oil

1 red onion, very thinly sliced

Freshly ground black pepper

Grated Parmesan cheese, preferably aged 24 months

CAPPUCCINO-CAPER PASTA

{ *Chitarra al caffè e capperi* }

SERVES *4 to 6* | **REGION:** *Veneto*

Creamy Parmesan and briny capers pair marvelously with coffee's rich, earthy aroma—it's like savory cappuccino on a fork!

Not convinced? Try tasting a caper and then a sip of coffee. Chef Heinz Beck, in his book *L'ingrediente Segreto*, writes about this pairing, "You'll be amazed by the lovely rich aftertaste of roasted hazelnuts, surprisingly pleasing." This seemingly bizarre combination of ingredients results in one of my favorite recipes. A must-try for any coffee lover!

Rinse the capers, removing all the salt, and squash them with the back of a wooden spoon. Set aside.

In a pan large enough to later toss the pasta, melt the butter over medium heat. Sprinkle in the flour, stirring until smooth, then slowly add in the milk, a little at a time, stirring constantly with a wooden spoon until smooth. Cook for 3 to 5 minutes on low, until the mixture is thickened; add the espresso to taste, and stir until well combined. Remove from the heat, add ½ cup (60 g) of Parmesan, and stir until the cheese is melted. Season with salt and white pepper.

Meanwhile, boil the pasta in salted water until it is al dente. Drain and toss into the sauce until well combined, adding a little of the cooking liquid if needed. Garnish with the capers.

¼ cup (35 g) salted capers, preferably large and Sicilian

3 tablespoons butter

1½ tablespoons all-purpose flour

1 cup (240 ml) whole milk, warmed

2 tablespoons freshly brewed hot espresso or strong coffee

Grated Parmesan cheese

Salt and white pepper

1 pound (455 g) whole-wheat *maccheroni alla chitarra* or other pasta

PASTA WITH SEA URCHINS & COFFEE

{ *Tagliatelle con ricci di mare e caffè* }

SERVES 4 | **REGION:** *Lombardy*

1 pound (455 g) tagliatelle, linguine, or other long pasta

Salt

12 small or 4 large sea urchins (about 6 ounces (180 g) sea urchin meat)

Olive oil

2 teaspoons finely ground espresso

Early mornings when I'm in Sicily, I go down to the docks to buy my favorite breakfast—sea urchins on crusty bread. Just like the craggy fishermen there do, I wash it down with an espresso.

Since I've long associated sea urchins with espresso, it didn't shock me when Chef Carlo Cracco, whose Milan restaurant is on *Restaurant* magazine's "World's 50 Best Restaurants" list, introduced the pairing with pasta. "It's a pleasing combination because the acidity of the coffee replaces the lemon that's usually paired with sea urchins," he explains.

Boil the pasta in salted water until it is al dente. Drain, and reserve some of the cooking water.

Open the sea urchins and remove the meat. In a skillet large enough to later toss the pasta, cook the sea urchins with 2 tablespoons oil over medium heat for about 1 minute, until they begin to dissolve a bit. Toss the pasta into the pan, adding a few tablespoons of the pasta cooking water, until well combined. Serve the pasta topped with the espresso. If you like, you can serve the pasta in the sea urchin shells!

CHAPTER

8

Fresh Pasta

CONTI CORTI E TAGLIATELLE LUNGHE.

BILLS SHOULD BE SMALL AND TAGLIATELLE LONG.

A popular saying in Bologna, a city renowned for its tagliatelle.

I obviously love pasta, but the truth is, I almost never used to make it from scratch. Why? I have two kids and a husband, and it takes a lot of kneading to make enough pasta to feed four! Then I learned something fantastic in Bologna: Have everyone make their own pasta portion. If you don't have to deal with a ton of dough, you might have more incentive to try your hand at fresh pasta.

Italians have a perfect ratio for making one serving of fresh pasta: 100 grams of flour (3.5 ounces, or about ¾ cup) and one large egg. The size of the dough ball is really manageable this small, so it quickly takes on that nice, silky, elastic quality. Try making tagliatelle or another pasta using this simple ratio—each guest can be in charge of mixing, kneading, rolling out, and cutting their own pasta!

In this chapter, you'll discover some wonderfully chubby, wobbly pasta that's as easy to make as playing with playdough—no need for paper-thin perfection. Many of the recipes, like World's Easiest Pasta (page 165), Crunchy Cornmeal-Buckwheat Triangles (page 155), and Little Chestnut Gnocchi (page 148) are easy enough for a four-year-old!

SARDINIAN PASTA RINGS WITH MINT, TOMATOES, & BOTTARGA

{ *Lorighittas* }

SERVES 4 | **REGION:** *Sardinia, especially the town of Morgongiori*

FOR THE PASTA:

2 cups (250 g) all-purpose or "o" flour

FOR THE SAUCE:

Salt

Olive oil

2 pints (570 g) grape or cherry tomatoes

2 garlic cloves

¼ cup (25 g) thinly sliced fresh mint

FOR SERVING:

1 ounce (30 g) *bottarga* (dried fish roe) or aged pecorino cheese, optional

Freshly ground black pepper

Lorighittas are adorable twirled rings of pasta found only in Sardinia. Legend has it that *lorighittas* were invented by a man who, finally after winning over his lover's heart, created this pretty ring-shaped pasta in celebration.

Making them is very relaxing, but it takes time. I love serving them to guests, but instead of making them all myself, I knead the dough in advance and then portion out little handfuls and have everyone fashion their own. It's a fun activity for family or friends and doesn't involve any special equipment, not even a knife. Just pinch off a bit of dough, roll it into thin strings, loop a couple of times, and twist. You'll taste how special they are in every bite.

Pomodori schiattarisciati, Pugliese dialect for "bursting tomatoes," are often served in a bowl accompanied by crusty bread as a communally shared starter, but here it's used as a sauce. If you like, top the pasta with flavorful grated *bottarga*—dried fish roe that's also a specialty of Sardinia.

Make the pasta: Mound the flour onto a work surface and make a well in the center. Slowly pour in ¼ cup (60 ml) warm water, whisking with a fork to incorporate it into the flour. Add more water, a little at a time, until a dough forms. Knead the dough until it is very smooth, about 10 minutes. Form it into a ball, cover with plastic wrap, and let the dough rest at room temperature for 1 hour.

recipe continues

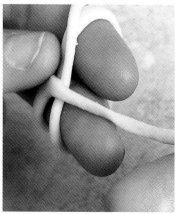

Working with a small handful of dough at a time so it doesn't dry out and keeping the rest covered, roll the dough into a long strand about ¼ inch (6 mm) thick. It's easiest if you roll the dough on a smooth surface like a stainless-steel table. Pinch off about 9 inches (23 cm) of the strand and loop it very loosely twice around the tips of two or three fingers. Make one loop slightly longer than the other. Then, with your thumb and fingertips, gently twist the two loops together, like you're winding a watch, until they are wrapped around each other, and press lightly to attach. Set the loops onto a cotton cloth.

Repeat until you've finished using all the dough. (If you are having trouble with the traditional method of looping it around three fingers, you can instead cut two lengths of about 5 inches (12 cm) each. Connect them at one end and gently twirl them until they are wrapped around each other. Then pinch the ends together to make an oval loop.)

Bring a large pot of salted water to a boil, and boil the pasta until it is al dente, about 3 to 6 minutes, depending on how thick your strands of dough are.

Make the sauce: Heat 3 tablespoons of oil in a small saucepan over high heat until it is very hot. Carefully put in the tomatoes, cover, and cook until you hear the distinctive "pops" of the skins bursting, about 4 minutes. Reduce the heat to medium and add the garlic. Cook for 2 minutes, until the garlic is light golden. Take it off the heat, remove the garlic, and stir in the mint.

To serve: Drain the pasta and toss it with the sauce. Serve it topped with grated or thinly shaved *bottarga* or pecorino cheese and season to taste with salt and pepper.

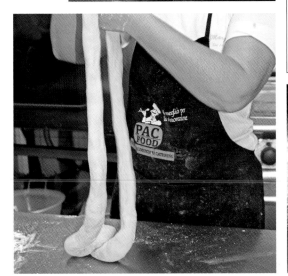

ITALY'S HUGE RINGS: PASTA ALLA MUGNAIA

Lorighittas are not the only ring-shaped pasta found in Italy! *Pasta alla Mugnaia*—a continuous ring of amazingly thick pasta—is hands-down the most unusual pasta I've ever eaten.

A mound of flour, enough to feed six, is worked into one humongous ring-shaped loop as thick as your thumb. It's wonderfully irregular, as some parts of the dough are rolled and some stretched and so thick that it has to be boiled twice to fully cook. This specialty of the Pescara province of Abruzzo is served with a rich pork-and-lamb ragù and presented to the table in one giant mound. Locals all claim the best place to eat it is in the tiny town of Elice, and my favorite restaurant there is Ristorante da Margherita. Go on a Saturday or, better yet, Sunday, and see long tables of friends all sharing massive platters. The pasta is so unusual, so toothsome and delicious, that I'm planning my next vacation around a second helping.

SWEET LEMON-MARJORAM RAVIOLI

{ Ravioli dolci }

SERVES 4; *makes about* **40** *ravioli* | **REGION:** *Abruzzo, especially the Teramo area*

FOR THE FILLING:

1¾ cups (435 g) ricotta

⅓ to ½ cup (65 to 100 g) sugar

2 to 3 tablespoons rum

Zest of ½ lemon

2 teaspoons fresh marjoram

Pinch ground cinnamon

1 large egg yolk

FOR THE DOUGH:

About 3½ cups (445 g) all-purpose or "o" flour

4 large eggs

Olive oil

FOR SERVING:

3 cups (720 ml) fresh tomato sauce or pork ragù (page 172), warmed

Parmesan or pecorino cheese

This is one of my all-time favorite recipes—very unusual and exceptionally flavorful. Savory-sweet ricotta ravioli seasoned with marjoram, lemon, rum, and sugar are a unique specialty from the Teramo area of Abruzzo.

The touch of sugar and rum in the filling brings out the marjoram's lovely aroma, while lemon zest adds a bright pop, all nicely balanced with the acidity of the sauce. The taste hearkens back to the Renaissance, when sweet and savory flavors were more commonly mixed. These must-try ravioli are traditionally served in a fresh tomato sauce or pork ragù.

If you are new to ravioli making, make larger ravioli by rolling the dough a little thicker and putting more filling in the center. Italians call these huge ravioli *ravioloni*. This version is too good not to try.

Make the filling: In a large bowl, gently stir together the ricotta, sugar, rum, zest, marjoram, and cinnamon until just combined. Taste and adjust the seasonings, adding more sugar or rum to taste, then stir in the yolk. Do not overmix or the ricotta will become runny. Cover and refrigerate until ready to use.

Make the dough: Put the flour into a large bowl or on a work surface and make a well in the center. Beat the eggs with ½ teaspoon oil and add them to the well; slowly incorporate the egg mixture into the flour with your fingers until it forms a dough. You may need to add a little water if the dough seems too dry or a little flour if it is sticky. Knead for at least 5 minutes, until smooth. Form the dough into a ball, cover with plastic wrap, and let it rest at room temperature for 30 minutes.

Using a quarter of the dough at a time so it doesn't dry out and keeping the rest covered, roll the dough into a sheet about ¹⁄₁₆ inch (2 mm) thick. Cut the sheet into two equal strips and put rounded tablespoons of filling along the center of one strip, leaving 1½ inches (4 cm) between dollops. Moisten around the filling with a little water, top with the other strip of dough, and press the two pieces of dough together around the filling, so the filling is sealed inside. Using a pasta-cutting wheel or ravioli cutter, cut out the ravioli in squares or rounds, leaving a ½-inch (12-mm) border around the filling. Repeat with the remaining dough and filling, setting them onto a clean cotton cloth in one layer.

To serve: Bring one or two wide, flat pans of salted water to a gentle boil and cook the ravioli until they are tender, about 4 minutes. Remove them with a slotted spoon to serving plates, and top with a few tablespoons of warm sauce and grated cheese.

IL BOCCONE DELLA VERGOGNA

In Italy, it's considered polite to leave one bite on your plate as a sign that you're full. Otherwise, an Italian host is likely to just keep giving you more food! It's also customary at a restaurant, when you are served from a communal platter, to leave one morsel. However, if the food is exceptionally delicious, too good to leave any behind, an Italian will take the last bit, and eat it with great flourish, calling it *il boccone della vergogna*, "the mouthful of shame." It's a very common expression, a sort of ironic apology for the breach of etiquette, and is intended as a compliment to the cook.

LITTLE CHESTNUT GNOCCHI

{ Gnocchetti di castagne }

SERVES 4 | **REGION:** *Northern Italy, especially the mountains of Liguria and Lombardy*

FOR THE GNOCCHETTI:

5 large fresh chestnuts

½ large russet potato

1 large egg

1 large egg yolk

Salt

3 to 4 tablespoons all-purpose or "o" flour

FOR THE SAUCE:

8 ounces (225 g) taleggio or *robiola* cheese, diced

1 to 2 tablespoons milk or cream

Freshly ground black pepper

Fresh thyme leaves

Grated Parmesan cheese

Leave it to the Italians to transform fifteen chestnuts and half a potato into a gourmet feast for four!

Satisfyingly chewy and permeated with chestnutty sweetness, these adorable little *gnocchetti* are denser and more complex tasting than the all-potato versions. Plus, as with all gnocchi, you just need to roll the dough into a chunky rope. Making them is a great way to get in touch with your inner child—more like playing with playdough than cooking!

The simply made aromatic cream sauce adds nice acidity, complementing the chestnut's sweetness. Special thanks to Sonia Piscicelli and her delightful daughter Emma for the recipe and photos.

Make the gnocchetti: Boil the chestnuts in their shells for about 30 minutes, until they feel soft, then remove the shells and skin from the chestnuts while they are still warm. (Quick tip: Since they don't need to stay whole, you don't have to be neat about peeling them. Cut them in half, and scoop out the meat with a spoon.) Mash the chestnuts with a fork or put them through a food mill and set aside.

Boil the potato until tender, then peel and mash it. Put the chestnut puree and half the mashed potato in a bowl and add the egg, yolk, and a pinch of salt and knead, adding in the flour a little at a time, until a soft dough forms. Divide the dough into four pieces and roll each into a ½-inch- (12-mm-) thick log. Cut the logs into hazelnut-sized pieces, then roll each into a tiny ball. Using your pinkie or the tip of a spoon, press a well into the center of each ball. You should get about eighty gnocchetti.

Boil the *gnochetti* in plenty of salted water until they float to the top and are tender, about 4 minutes. Drain.

Make the sauce: In a small pan, combine the cheese and milk and heat over low heat, stirring often. Spoon some of the cheese sauce onto each serving plate and top with the gnocchetti. Serve sprinkled with pepper, thyme, and Parmesan.

PANCAKE PASTA

{ Testaroli }

SERVES 4 | REGION: *Liguria and Tuscany*

½ cup (55 g) all-purpose or "o" flour

½ cup (about 85 g) whole-wheat, fine cornmeal, or other flour

Olive oil

Salt

½ onion

¾ cup (180 ml) pesto or grated pecorino cheese

I had no clue what to make of the eighteen-inch giant spongy pancake I spotted in a gourmet shop in Liguria. It was shrink-wrapped, rolled like a diploma, and tied with pretty green ribbon. When the shopkeeper explained that it was a "pasta," meant to be boiled, I was dubious. I mean, who would boil a pancake? Turns out, the Italians have been doing it since as early as the 1300s, and perhaps even back in ancient Roman times.

The name of this pasta, *testaroli*, derives from *testo*, the special terra-cotta pan these pancakes are cooked in. Of course, you can make them in a cast-iron skillet or other pans as well. The dough is simple to work with, more like crêpe pancake batter than pasta dough. In Italy, they combine all kinds of flours with white flour to make the batter: whole-wheat, fine cornmeal, buckwheat, farro, and chestnut flours. So here's a good chance to try a new flour you've been wanting to experiment with.

This is a great make-ahead dish, as the pasta pancakes are best after they've rested overnight and will stay fresh for a week before boiling. Try them topped with any of the pesto recipes like delicious Orange-Almond Pesto (page 111) or the aromatic marjoram version (page 54).

In a large bowl, combine the flours. Add 1½ tablespoons oil, 1 teaspoon salt, and slowly stir in 2 cups (480 ml) water to get a thin, smooth mixture, like crêpe batter. Let it rest at room temperature for 10 minutes.

Heat a large nonstick sauté pan, cast-iron skillet, or crêpe pan over medium heat. Dip the onion half into some oil and rub it onto the pan to grease the surface and flavor the oil a bit. Add just enough batter to the pan to create a thin layer, spreading it quickly by tilting the pan, just as you would when making crêpes. Cook until the edges come up a bit and you can easily turn over the pancake, about 7 to 10 minutes. Turn and cook it on the other side for about 5 minutes. Remove it to a clean surface

*Come il cacio sui
maccheroni*

———

Like cheese on pasta

SAID OF SOMETHING THAT'S
ESPECIALLY WONDERFUL

and allow to cool. Repeat, remoistening the pan with the oil-dipped onion, until all the batter is used. Then once the pancakes are cool and dry to the touch, stack them between waxed or parchment paper in an airtight container in a cool place for at least 12 hours before cooking or they will be gummy.

To cook the pancakes, cut them into 2-bite rectangles or triangles. Bring a pot of salted water to a boil, add the pancake pieces, and immediately turn off the heat. Leave them in the water for 2 to 3 minutes, until they are tender. Drain and serve them topped with pesto or a drizzle of oil and grated pecorino.

PUGLIA'S TWIRLED PASTA WITH OLIVES

{ Incannulate con olive }

SERVES 4 | REGION: *Puglia*

FOR THE SAUCE:

30 *Cerignola* or other large green olives

10 oil-cured small black olives

Olive oil

15 fresh mint leaves, minced

3 tablespoons homemade coarsely ground breadcrumbs, toasted

Grated aged pecorino cheese

2 tablespoons fresh oregano leaves

1 tablespoon white wine vinegar

1 garlic clove, minced

Salt and freshly ground black pepper

FOR THE PASTA:

2 cups (255 g) all-purpose or "o" flour

An adorable shape that's not at all hard to make—these long ribbons of wide noodle are twirled at one end, forming Shirley Temple–like curls. I learned to make this charming pasta in Puglia at the home of Lucia Contrada and Pasquali Galluccio, who orchestrated a memorable day when they also taught me to make other specialty shapes of that region like orecchiette.

Throughout southern Italy, olives are served fried, baked, and also stuffed. Here, the traditional olive filling with cheese, breadcrumbs, and herbs is instead a no-cook sauce for this pretty pasta.

Make the sauce: Using a meat mallet or fork, press down on the olives to smash them open. Remove and discard the pits. Put the olives into a serving bowl and stir in ¼ cup (60 ml) oil, the mint, breadcrumbs, 3 tablespoons cheese, the oregano, vinegar, and garlic. Season to taste with salt and pepper. Cover with plastic wrap and let the mixture rest at room temperature while you make the pasta.

Make the pasta: Put the flour onto a work surface. Make a well in the center and add ¼ cup (60 ml) warm water. Using a fork, slowly incorporate the flour into the water, starting from the center, until a dough forms. Add a few additional tablespoons of water at a time as needed, until you've incorporated it all into the flour. Knead the dough until smooth, about 8 minutes. Form it into a ball, cover with plastic wrap, and let it rest at room temperature for 30 minutes.

Roll out the dough into a large circle about ⅛ inch (6 mm) thick. Cut it into strips ¾ inch (2 cm) wide. Hold one end of a strip with one hand and twirl the other end with your other hand, like you are winding a watch, then gently pinch both ends to keep them from uncurling. Double the twist over loosely, forming a "u," and set it out onto a cotton cloth or floured surface. Repeat using the rest of the dough.

To serve: Boil the pasta in salted water until it is al dente, about 3 minutes. Drain and toss into the bowl with the olive mixture. Top with more grated cheese, if you like.

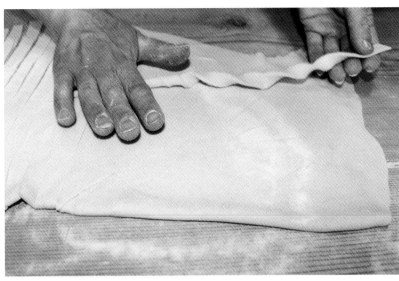

CRUNCHY CORNMEAL-BUCKWHEAT TRIANGLES

{ Blécs }

SERVES 4 | REGION: *Friuli*

Blécs are one of the easiest homemade pastas to tackle. The wholesome buckwheat-cornmeal dough is thickly rolled out and rough cut into irregular-shaped triangles. The name in fact is dialect for a bit of cloth for patching. The sauce is unique, too—a crunchy cornmeal mixture seasoned with sage and topped with smoky grated cheese. Be sure to use finely ground cornmeal for both the dough and the sauce.

Make the blécs: In a large bowl or on a work surface, mix the buckwheat, all-purpose, and corn flours. Make a well in the center and add the eggs, 3 tablespoons oil, and the salt. Combine the wet ingredients first, then slowly incorporate the flour into the liquid, adding a little water as needed, until a dough forms. Cover the dough with plastic wrap, and let rest it at room temperature for 30 minutes.

On a lightly floured surface, roll out the dough to about ⅛ inch (2 mm) thick and cut it into 2-inch (5-cm) triangles.

Put the bay leaf in a large pot of salted water and bring it to a boil. Add the blécs and boil until tender, about 3 minutes.

To finish: In a nonstick skillet large enough to later toss the *blécs*, melt the butter and a few sage leaves. Once the butter is bubbly and the sage aromatic, remove the sage to use as garnish and sprinkle in the cornmeal, stirring with a wooden spoon over medium heat until it is crunchy and golden colored. Season with salt and pepper.

Drain the *blécs*, discard the bay leaf, and toss the pasta into the cornmeal mixture. Serve it topped with the cheese and reserved buttery sage leaves.

FOR THE BLÉCS:

¾ cup (115 g) buckwheat flour

¾ cup (90 g) all-purpose or "o" flour

¾ cup (105 g) fine-grind yellow cornmeal

2 large eggs

Olive oil

¼ teaspoon salt

1 bay leaf

FOR FINISHING:

4 tablespoons (60 g) butter

Fresh sage leaves

2 tablespoons fine-grind yellow cornmeal

Salt and freshly ground black pepper

1 cup (100 g) grated smoked ricotta or Gouda cheese

APPLE RAVIOLI WITH FAVA-PISTACHIO PESTO

{ *Ravioli di mele con pesto di fave-pistacchi* }

SERVES 4 | **REGION:** *Northern and central Italy*

FOR THE PESTO:

1 cup (120 g) shelled fresh fava beans or ¼ cup (50 g) dried fava beans

⅓ cup (40 g) shelled pistachios

2 tablespoons pine nuts

About 30 large fresh basil leaves

Olive oil

Salt and freshly ground black pepper

FOR THE DOUGH:

3½ cups (445 g) all-purpose or "o" flour

4 large eggs

Olive oil

1 large egg white

FOR THE FILLING:

2 tablespoons butter

3 Granny Smith apples, peeled and diced

5 to 7 fresh sage leaves

1 pound (455 g) *robiola* or taleggio cheese, diced

Chestnut or buckwheat honey

If you try no other recipe in this chapter, try this one. The apple, honey, and cheese filling is simply astounding and the addition of fava beans to the pistachios makes for a smoky, sweet, richly satisfying pesto. Don't be intimidated by the idea of making your own ravioli. For this recipe, because the filling is so dense, the dough doesn't need to be thin. These ravioli are also oversized, so cut them into fairly large circles with a cookie cutter and they will be easy to fill.

My son liked this recipe so much that he arranged for me to come up to his college during his senior year to make it with a bunch of his favorite professors. He graduated summa cum laude—thanks to these ravioli, I'm sure!

Make the pesto: Boil the fresh beans in salted water until tender, about 4 minutes (simmer about 45 minutes for dried). Drain, peel, and pat dry. In a small food processor or mortar and pestle, grind the beans, pistachios, and pine nuts until very smooth. Add the basil and then, while processing, slowly stream in ¼ cup (60 ml) oil, grinding until creamy, adding more oil if dry. Season to taste with salt and pepper.

Make the dough: Put the flour in a large bowl or on a work surface and make a well in the center. Beat the whole eggs and 1 teaspoon oil into the well with a fork. Gradually incorporate the flour until a dough forms. Knead the dough until it is very smooth, at least 5 minutes. Form it into a ball, cover with plastic wrap, and let the dough rest at room temperature for 30 minutes.

Make the filling: In a sauté pan, melt the butter over high heat. Add the apples and sage and cook until the apples are just tender, but still a bit firm. Let them cool to room temperature.

To *assemble:* Using a quarter of the dough at a time so it doesn't dry out and keeping the rest covered, roll the dough into ⅛-inch- (3-mm-) thick sheets either with a rolling pin or pasta machine. Using a cookie or ravioli cutter, cut to 4-inch (10-cm) circles. Beat the egg white in a bowl to use for sealing the ravioli.

Put 1 tablespoon of the apple mixture onto a dough circle, then top with 1 tablespoon of the cheese and a tiny drizzle of honey. Moisten the edges of the dough with the egg white, top with another dough circle, and press the edges firmly to seal. Repeat until all the dough and filling are used.

Bring one or two wide, flat pans of salted water to a gentle boil and cook the ravioli until they are tender. Remove them with a slotted spoon to serving plates. Serve topped with dollops of the pesto.

TORTELLI WITH A TAIL

{ Tortelli Piacentini con la coda }

SERVES 4 **|** REGION: *Emilia-Romagna, especially the province of Piacenza*

FOR THE FILLING:

1 shallot, finely minced

Olive oil

8 ounces (225 g) peas

3 to 4 thin stalks asparagus, thinly sliced

2 tablespoons finely sliced oil-packed sun dried tomatoes

Salt and freshly ground black pepper

1 cup (250 g) ricotta

Grated Parmesan cheese

1 large egg

2 tablespoons pine nuts, chopped

4 to 5 fresh basil leaves, minced

FOR THE DOUGH:

2 cups (255 g) all-purpose or "o" flour

3 large eggs

Olive oil

FOR SERVING:

3 tablespoons butter

4 to 5 fresh sage leaves

Grated Parmesan cheese

The filling for these charming bundles—ricotta, peas, asparagus, sun-dried tomatoes, and pine nuts—is so good you'll be tempted to eat it right out of the bowl! But be sure to save some to make these unique tortelli, which are fun to fold into their unique cocoonlike shape. They don't have to be perfect to be delicious. They are served here topped with a simple combo of melted butter, sage, and grated cheese.

This specialty of Emilia-Romagna was invented in the mid-1300s in honor of famed poet Francesco Petrarch, who was visiting a nobleman in Piacenza.

Make the filling: In a medium pan, cook the shallot in 1 tablespoon oil over medium heat until it is softened, about 1 minute. Stir in the peas, asparagus, and tomatoes, cover, and cook until tender, about 7 minutes. Lightly mash the vegetables with a potato masher; season to taste with salt and pepper. In a bowl combine the ricotta, ⅓ cup (40 g) of Parmesan, egg, pine nuts, and basil with the cooled vegetable mixture. Refrigerate until ready to use.

Make the dough: Put the flour onto a work surface. Make a well in the center and beat the eggs and ½ teaspoon oil into the well with a fork. Slowly incorporate the flour into the eggs until a dough forms, adding a few tablespoons of water if it is dry. Knead the dough until it is very smooth, about 5 minutes. Form it into a ball, cover with plastic wrap, and let the dough rest at room temperature for 30 minutes.

Roll out the dough about ⅛ inch (3 mm) thick. Using a cookie or ravioli cutter, cut 4-inch (10-cm) circles. Put a heaping tablespoon of the filling in the center of a circle and fold down about ¼ inch (6 mm) of the top edge of the dough. Then fold a little of the top left corner down over the center, then a little of the right corner over that. Continue folding in alternate sides, moving down the center until you reach the end of the dough circle. Pinch closed the "tail." Repeat with the remaining dough and filling.

To serve: Boil the tortelli in one layer in two wide pans of salted water until they are tender, about 4 minutes. Meanwhile, melt the butter with the sage in a small saucepan until the butter browns a bit, about 2 minutes. Remove the tortelli using a slotted spoon and serve them drizzled with the sage butter and topped with cheese.

"KNITTING NEEDLE" PASTA WITH FRIED PEPPERS

{ Pasta al ceppo }

SERVES 4 | REGION: *Abruzzo, Puglia, and southern Italy*

FOR THE SAUCE:

Olive oil

16 baby bell peppers or 4 large bell peppers, a mix of red, yellow, and green

2 garlic cloves, sliced

¼ cup (60 ml) *vino cotto* or sweet Marsala wine

Fresh minced parsley

Salt and freshly ground black pepper

FOR THE PASTA:

2 cups (255 g) all-purpose or "0" flour

FOR SERVING

Grated pecorino cheese

This specialty of Abruzzo is called *pasta al ceppo*, after the wooden knitting needles that the dough was originally wrapped around to create its distinctive shape. In other parts of southern Italy, this same type of pasta was wrapped around a metal rod and called by various names, including *pasta col ferretto*, pasta with iron. Although there are specialty devices for making this pasta, many home cooks still use knitting needles, or even the spokes from umbrellas!

I was taught this fun-to-make shape at the home of Tiziana Ragusi, who arranged for her seventeen-year-old son Roberto Paolini, his grandmother Margherita Palumbi, and three friends to teach me. The first few I made got squashed as I pulled them off the rod, so don't get discouraged. They're tasty even when squashed!

Make the sauce: In a large sauté pan, heat 3 to 4 tablespoons oil over medium-high heat until very hot. Add the whole baby peppers (or seeded and quartered large peppers) and cook until they are dark golden on one side, about 3 minutes. Turn the peppers over, lower the heat to medium, and add the garlic and wine. Cook until the wine evaporates and the peppers are very soft, about 5 minutes. Season to taste with salt and pepper. Remove the pan from the heat and top the peppers with a sprinkling of parsley. Let them rest at room temperature while you make the pasta.

Make the pasta: Put the flour onto a work surface. Make a well in the center and add ¼ cup (60 ml) warm water. Using a fork, slowly incorporate the flour into the water, starting from the center, until a dough forms. Add a few tablespoons of water at a time if the dough is dry. Knead it until very smooth, about 8 minutes. Form the dough into a ball, cover it with plastic wrap, and let it rest at room temperature for 30 minutes.

Roll the dough into a ½-inch- (12-mm-) thick strand. Cut off a 2-inch (5-cm) section. Put a metal rod or knitting needle in the center of the dough section and use your palm to gently roll it in one motion until the dough is wrapped about the rod. Gently pull the pasta off the rod. Set the pasta out in a single layer onto a cotton cloth or floured surface. Repeat using the rest of the dough.

To serve: Boil the pasta in salted water until it is al dente, about 4 minutes. Drain and toss with the peppers. Serve topped with grated cheese. (In Italy, they serve the baby peppers stems and all, which are then cut off on the plate with the edge of a fork, or even picked up by the stem and bitten off. The discarded stems are left at the edge of the plate.)

FRUIT & HERB "PANTS"

{ Cjalsons }

SERVES 6 | REGION: *Friuli–Venezia Giulia, especially Carnia*

FOR THE FILLING:

3 tablespoons raisins or currants

2 tablespoons grappa or rum

1 pound (455 g) Idaho or russet potatoes

5 tablespoons (70 g) butter

1 cup (100 g) minced assorted fresh herbs like parsley, mint, marjoram, and basil

1 small pear, peeled and grated

1 small apple, peeled and grated

½ cup (60 g) grated smoked ricotta or Gouda

2 tablespoons apricot or cherry jam

2 tablespoons homemade breadcrumbs, toasted, or crushed amaretti cookies

Zest of 1 lemon

1 teaspoon cocoa powder or grated dark chocolate

1 teaspoon ground cinnamon, plus extra for garnish

Salt

Of all the weird but wonderful recipes in this book, this is one of the weirdest and most wonderful!

These savory half-moon bundles are filled with an astonishing array of ingredients: mashed potatoes, smoked cheese, lots of herbs, spices, and fruit—including apples, pears, apricot jam, raisins, lemon zest, and, yes, even chocolate! They date to the Middle Ages and were renowned, even then, for the many aromatic herbs and numerous spices included in the filling.

Cjalsons—pants, in the local dialect—get that name from their chubby horseshoe shape, which resembles a pair of cowboy chaps or baggy pants.

Make the filling: Soak the raisins in the grappa until they are soft, about 30 minutes.

In a pot of boiling water, cook the potatoes until tender. Transfer the potatoes to a large bowl and mash them until smooth. Mix in 2 tablespoons of the butter until it is melted, then add the raisins and any remaining liquor, the herbs, pear, apple, 6 tablespoons (45 g) of the cheese, the jam, breadcrumbs, zest, cocoa, cinnamon, and salt to taste and mix until well combined. Set the mixture aside to allow the flavors to meld while you make the dough.

Make the dough: Put the flour in a large bowl and make a well in the center. Beat the eggs in the well with a fork. Gradually incorporate the flour into the eggs, adding about ½ cup (120 ml) warm water, until a dough forms. Knead until it is elastic. Let the dough rest in the bowl, covered with a damp cotton cloth, for 30 minutes.

Using a quarter of the dough at a time so it doesn't dry out, and keeping the rest covered, roll the dough into ⅛-inch- (3-mm-) thick sheets. Using a cookie or ravioli cutter, cut 3½- to 4-inch (9- to 10-cm) circles. You should get about 36 circles.

Place a heaping tablespoonful of filling in the center of each circle of dough, moisten the edges with water or egg white, then fold and press the edges closed to make half moons; pinch each one in the center to resemble chubby cowboy chaps.

In one or two wide pans, in a single layer, boil the *cjalsons* in salted water until they are tender, about 5 minutes. Meanwhile, in a small saucepan, melt the remaining butter. Remove the *cjalsons* with a slotted spoon to serving plates. Drizzle each serving with the melted butter and top with the remaining cheese and a pinch of cinnamon.

FOR THE DOUGH:

3½ cups (445 g) all-purpose or "o" flour

3 large eggs

1 large egg white, lightly beaten, optional

ONCE UPON A TIME

The legend about *cjalsons* claims that once upon a time, the valleys and mountains of Friuli were filled with goblins called *sbilfs*. Guriut, one of the most greedy and mischievous of them, was caught one night stealing cream as it floated to the surface of a bucket of fresh milk. The milkmaid tried to trap him in a large basket, but Guriut was too quick for her and, grabbing her skirt, made her drop the basket. He then began covering her in tender kisses and caresses, which so pleased the milkmaid that they became lovers. As a reward for releasing him, Guriut taught her his secret recipe for *cjalsons*.

WORLD'S EASIEST PASTA

{ Frascarelli }

SERVES 4 | **REGION:** *le Marche and throughout central and southern Italy, with variations found also in the northern Trentino–Alto Adige region*

You don't need any special equipment to make this pasta—just your own nimble fingers. Spread flour onto a work surface, sprinkle it with a few drops of water, and stir and pinch it to form tiny nuggets.

The name of this pasta, *frascarelli*, comes from the Italian for "twigs"—little bundles of dried oregano or rosemary stems traditionally used to sprinkle the drops of water into the flour. The cooked frascarelli were eaten right off the wooden board used to make the pasta, and they're still classically served that way in Italy.

This was a "poor" dish, often served with just a drizzle of olive oil and bit of grated cheese. That said, these tender, rustic nuggets are absolutely fabulous topped with savory sausage and pecorino cheese.

4 cups (680 g) semolina flour

2 large eggs

1 rosemary branch (optional)

Salt

Olive oil

3 sweet sausages

Pecorino cheese

Spread the flour onto a large wooden board. In a small bowl, beat the eggs with ½ cup (120 ml) water. Drip the egg mixture onto the flour a little at a time, using a fork or the rosemary branch, and stir with your fingertips to form little nuggets. As they form, pick the resulting nuggets out of the flour and into a mesh sifter. Shake off any excess flour and transfer the nuggets onto a cotton dishcloth. Repeat until the egg mixture is used up, adding more flour if needed. Let the nuggets air dry, uncovered, for 2 hours.

Bring 1 quart (960 ml) lightly salted water to a boil and add the pasta nuggets. Reduce the heat to medium and simmer for about 10 minutes, stirring occasionally, until they are tender.

Meanwhile, in a small sauté pan, heat 2 tablespoons oil over medium-high heat. Remove the meat from the sausage casings, add it to the pan, and cook until it is lightly browned, breaking up the meat with a wooden spoon as it cooks.

Once the pasta is tender, spread it out onto a serving platter or wooden board, and top with the sausage and a generous sprinkling of shaved or grated cheese and a drizzle of oil.

9

Holidays

A NATALE CON I TUOI E A PASQUA CON CHI VUOI.
SPEND CHRISTMAS WITH YOUR FAMILY,
BUT EASTER WITH WHOMEVER YOU WANT.
A popular expression throughout Italy.

Every region in Italy has special foods associated with the country's many different holidays. In this chapter, you'll discover delicious Christmastime specialties, including Christmas Eve Almond-Milk Pasta (page 170), decadent Carnevale delights, as well as the special Sicilian Baked Easter Pasta (page 175), a lovely make-ahead picnic dish traditionally eaten on *Pasquetta*, the day after Easter. You can even celebrate International Women's Day, on March 8th, with BFF Pasta (page 178).

FRUIT & NUT
CHRISTMAS EVE LASAGNE

{ Lasagne da fornel }

SERVES 6 | **REGION:** *Veneto and Friuli–Venezia Giulia*

8 to 10 dried white Calimyrna figs, thinly sliced

½ cup (120 ml) dry white wine

2 Red Delicious apples, grated

1 cup (145 g) golden raisins and/or dried cherries

1 cup (115 g) finely ground toasted walnuts

12 tablespoons butter (170 g), melted

1 pound (455 g) fresh egg-pasta lasagne sheets, cut into strips 3 inches (7.5 cm) wide, or any fresh wide-cut egg noodle

1 tablespoon poppy seeds

Seasoned with apples, dried fruit, poppy seeds, and nuts, this is a savory pasta version of apple strudel. This specialty from the Dolomite area of northern Italy is traditionally served as a first course on Christmas Eve.

In Italy, lasagne, the plural of lasagna, is a term that refers to pasta cut into wide strips, and the resulting dish is more free-form than what we in the States usually imagine when we think of cheesy, red-sauce lasagne.

Preheat the oven to 350°F (175°C). Generously butter a 9-inch (23-cm) ovenproof serving dish or baking pan.

In a small saucepan, combine the figs and wine and bring them to a boil over high heat. Boil for a minute or two, then reduce the heat to low and simmer until all the wine is absorbed, about 2 minutes. In a bowl, combine the apples, figs, raisins, walnuts, and half of the butter.

Boil the lasagne strips in salted water until they are al dente. Drain and toss with the remaining butter and the poppy seeds. In the prepared dish or pan, put down a single layer of lasagne strips haphazardly. Spread them with one third of the fruit mixture. Repeat for two more layers of noodles and fruit mixture. Top with a final layer of noodles. Bake for about 20 minutes, until the lasagne is hot throughout. Serve.

CHRISTMAS EVE ALMOND-MILK PASTA

{ Lasagnette all'ajada }

SERVES 4 | **REGION:** *Lombardy, Piedmont, and Liguria*

2 slices white bread, crusts removed

1 quart (960 ml) almond milk

Salt

1 pound (455 g) *lasagnette* or other wide noodles

½ cup (55 g) chopped toasted walnuts

2 garlic cloves

Olive oil

½ cup (56 g) homemade coarsely ground breadcrumbs, toasted

Wide noodles cooked in almond milk are then tossed in a dense walnut-garlic pesto and topped with toasted breadcrumbs. This is totally vegan, homey and comforting.

Delicious any time of year, this dish is traditionally served on Christmas Eve. *Lasagnette all'ajada* gets its name from how the pasta are cut, *ajada* style—in wide strips, meant to be evocative of a baby's swaddling.

Soak the bread in a few tablespoons of the almond milk until very soft.

Bring the rest of the milk and a little salt to a boil and cook the noodles in it until they are al dente. Drain.

Meanwhile, in a mortar and pestle or small food processor, finely grind the walnuts and garlic. Squeeze some of the excess liquid from the bread and grind the bread into the mixture. With the processor still running, slowly drizzle in a few tablespoons of oil, until the mixture is dense and creamy.

Heat 1 to 2 tablespoons oil in a pan and add the breadcrumbs; re-toast until they are crisp. (Be sure to use coarse, not finely ground, breadcrumbs.)

Toss the pasta with the pesto until well combined and serve it topped with the breadcrumbs.

EVERYTHING BUT THE KITCHEN SINK CHRISTMAS TORTELLI

{ Tortelli cremaschi }

SERVES **6** *to* **8** | REGION: *Lombardy, especially Cremona*

"My mother and grandmother made these *tortelli* every year, with us children each assigned a different task," recalls Matilda, the gracious home cook from Lombardy who taught me this recipe. "I still remember our shock at seeing so many disparate ingredients end up in the filling. But the biggest surprise came at the end, when our mother would add a crushed mint candy into the filling! She'd stress, whispering, that it was our secret ingredient and not to tell anyone."

Well, as it turns out, virtually every family in Lombardy whom I interviewed added a mint candy as their "secret" ingredient!

Make the filling: In a small sauté pan, melt 3 tablespoons of the butter over medium-high heat and re-toast the breadcrumbs until they are crunchy.

In a large bowl, combine the breadcrumbs, amaretti crumbs, 1 cup (115 g) cheese, the pear, raisins, mostarda, mostaccino, zest, mint candy, and nutmeg to taste. Add the egg and wine and mix until well combined. If the mixture is too dry, add a few more tablespoons of wine or water. Cover and refrigerate for 24 hours.

Make the dough: Put the flour into a bowl, make a well in the center, and beat the eggs and ¼ cup (60 ml) warm water in the well. Slowly incorporate the flour into the egg mixture, adding a little more water if needed, until a dough forms. Knead the dough until it is very smooth. Form it into a ball, cover it with plastic wrap, and let rest at room temperature for 1 hour.

Roll out the dough into a ⅛-inch (3-mm) sheet, either with a pasta maker or with a rolling pin. Using a cookie or ravioli cutter or a very sharp knife, cut the pasta sheets into 3-inch (7.5-cm) squares. Put 1 teaspoon filling in the center of each square and fold it diagonally to make a triangle, pressing the edges closed, then pinch the sealed sides to make three pleats (one at the point, and one on each side). Spread the triangles out onto a clean cotton cloth in a single layer.

Boil the tortelli in plenty of salted water until they are tender, about 5 minutes. Toss them with the remaining 4 tablespoons (60 g) butter and serve topped with cheese.

FOR THE FILLING:

7 tablespoons (100 g) butter

½ cup (56 g) homemade finely ground breadcrumbs, toasted

1⅔ cups (about 200 g) crushed amaretti cookies

Grated *grana padano* or Parmesan cheese

1 small pear, peeled and diced

½ cup (85 g) raisins

½ cup (120 ml) *mostarda* (candied fruit compote in spicy mustard syrup; see Sources, page 200), finely minced

1 *mostaccino* cookie or a few crisp ginger snap cookies, crushed

Zest of 1 lemon

1 hard mint candy, crushed

Freshly grated nutmeg

1 large egg

½ cup (120 ml) sweet Marsala wine

FOR THE DOUGH:

About 4¼ cups (545 g) all-purpose or "0" flour

3 large eggs

NEAPOLITAN CARNEVALE LASAGNE

{ Lasagne di Carnevale Napoletana }

SERVES 8 | REGION: *Campania, especially Naples*

Rich ricotta lasagne layered with tiny meatballs, plus all sorts of optional extras like salami, sausage, and even sliced boiled eggs—this dish is the unofficial symbol of *Carnevale*. Very lush and elaborate, it requires time and patience to prepare, beginning with the classic Neapolitan ragù, which must be cooked slowly over low heat. Locals call the method *pippiare*—an onomatopoetic word that hints at the sound of the sauce barely simmering, as one tiny bubble pops at a time.

I love the instructions the Neapolitans give to let the lasagne "rest and reflect" for half an hour before serving. All the layers settle and you end up with gorgeous slices!

FOR THE RAGÙ:

Olive oil

12 ounces (340 g) boneless pork loin, cut into 3 large chunks

4 lean pork ribs

2 sweet sausages

1 yellow onion, minced

1 cup (240 ml) red wine, preferably from the Alianico grape, a specialty of Campania

1 (28-ounce/800-g) can strained tomatoes, such as Pomi or Alice Nero brands

1 (6-ounce/170-g) can tomato paste

4 to 5 large fresh basil leaves

Salt and freshly ground black pepper

FOR THE MEATBALLS:

2 slices white sandwich bread, crusts removed

8 ounces (225 g) ground beef or pork

1 large egg

Grated Parmesan cheese

Peanut or sunflower oil

Make the ragù: In a large saucepan, heat 2 tablespoons oil over medium heat. Add the pork, ribs, and sausages and brown them on all sides. Add the onion and sauté it for 5 minutes, then add ¼ cup (60 ml) of the wine. Reduce the heat to very low, cover, and simmer until the wine is absorbed, about 40 minutes. Add another ¼ cup (60 ml) of the wine and let it absorb; repeat, adding ¼ cup (60 ml) wine every 40 minutes or so until all the wine is absorbed and the meat is tender, about 2 hours more. Add the tomatoes, tomato paste, and basil. Season to taste with salt and pepper. Simmer on very low heat, covered, for 2 more hours, stirring occasionally and adding hot water if needed. When the ragù is thick and flavorful, remove the meats to serve separately at another time.

Make the meatballs: Wet the bread with a little water, squeeze out the excess, and put the bread in a bowl with the beef, egg, 2 heaping tablespoons Parmesan, and salt and pepper to taste. Mix until combined. Form tiny hazelnut-sized meatballs, about ½ inch (12 mm) in diameter.

In a small saucepan, heat 2 inches (5 cm) oil over medium-high heat. Add the meatballs a few at a time, and fry until they are golden, about 1 minute. Drain on a paper towel–lined plate.

To assemble: Preheat the oven to 350°F (175°C).

Mix the ricotta with 1 cup (240 ml) of the ragù and the basil.

Boil the lasagne sheets in salted water until they are al dente. Drain and spread onto clean cotton dishcloths to cool and to prevent sticking.

For layer #1: spread ½ inch (12 mm) of ragù on the bottom of a deep-sided 14-inch (35.5-cm) lasagne baking pan and top with a layer of noodles. Dollop with half of the ricotta mixture and scatter with half of the meatballs and half of the sausage, salami, and eggs, if using. Top with half of the mozzarella, generous dollops of ragù, and 3 heaping tablespoons of the Parmesan.

For layer #2: add another layer of lasagne, dollop with the remaining ricotta mixture, and scatter with the remaining meatballs. Spread on a few ladlefuls of ragù, the remaining mozzarella, and the remaining sausage, salami, and eggs, if using. Top with 3 heaping tablespoons of the Parmesan and finish with a final layer of lasagne. Generously spread the top with ragù and 3 heaping tablespoons of the Parmesan.

Bake for 1 hour, finishing at 450°F (230°C) so the top browns at the edges. Let the lasagne rest for 30 minutes before slicing. Serve it topped with more ragù and with grated cheese on the side.

Serve the pork loin, ribs, and sausages from the ragù as a second course on another day.

TO ASSEMBLE:

1½ pounds (680 g) ricotta cheese

8 to 10 fresh basil leaves, shredded

1 pound (455 g) flat (non-curly) lasagne sheets, preferably Garofalo brand

1 sausage, cooked and sliced, optional

8 ounces (225 g) thinly sliced salami, optional

3 large hard-boiled eggs, sliced, optional

About 1 cup (115 g) grated Parmesan cheese

12 ounces (340 g) mozzarella, cut into small cubes

LASAGNE AS STAR

There are many versions of this ragù in Naples. Lina Wertmuller's 1990 film *Sabato, Domenica e Lunedì* starring Sophia Loren, is all about this Neapolitan sauce. The title refers to the fact that you buy the ingredients on Saturday, make the sauce on Sunday, and eat the leftovers on Monday. There's a great scene where the customers in a butcher shop get so worked up discussing the ragù that a fight breaks out over which is the correct recipe.

CARNEVALE MACCHERONI WITH FIVE HOLES

{ Maccheroni con cinque buchi }

SERVES 4 | **REGION:** *Sicily, especially the Catania province*

Olive oil

1 large yellow onion, finely minced

4 country-style lean pork ribs

4 sausages

8 ounces (225 g) pork rind

½ cup (120 ml) dry red wine

1 (28-ounce/800-g) can tomato puree

3 tablespoons tomato paste

1 bay leaf

Salt and freshly ground black pepper

1 pound (455 g) *maccheroni con cinque buchi*, preferably Poiatti brand, or any pasta

Parmesan cheese, grated

CARNEVALE FOODS

All the foods for *Carnevale* are over-the-top rich—lots of fried specialties, lots of luscious fatty meats—because it is the last hurrah before Lent, a forty-day period when many foods, including meat, are traditionally restricted. The word *Carnevale* probably comes from the Latin "carnem levare," to remove meat.

It just wouldn't be *Carnevale* in Sicily without a plate of this decadently rich pork ragù served on *Martedí Grasso*, Fat Tuesday. The sauce is flavored with pork rind and, while that's not essential, it *is* really sinfully delicious. Yes, it's rich, but heck—it's called Fat Tuesday for a reason!

This is traditionally served with short, fabulously thick pasta called *maccheroni con cinque buchi*, which has one large hole in the center and four smaller holes around it. It's very toothsome and pretty, but if you can't find it, you can of course substitute any pasta shape.

In a large saucepan, heat 2 tablespoons oil over medium-high heat. Add the onion and sauté until it is golden and very soft, about 15 minutes. Add the ribs and whole sausages and brown them on all sides.

Meanwhile, bring a small pot of water to a boil and blanch the pork rind for a few minutes, then drain and cut into thick strips. Add the rind and wine to the meats and bring them to a low boil to burn off a bit of the alcohol. Stir in the tomato puree, tomato paste, and bay leaf and turn down the heat; simmer over very low heat, covered, for 3 hours. Season with salt and pepper.

Boil the pasta in salted water until it is al dente and drain. As in Sicily, you can serve this one of two ways: with the pasta tossed with just the sauce as a first course and the meats served as a second course, or as a more substantial pasta course, with pieces of the meat cut into small pieces right on the same plate with the pasta and sauce. In either version, be sure to serve the pasta topped with lots of grated cheese.

SICILIAN BAKED EASTER PASTA

{ *Taganu d'Aragona* }

SERVES 6 *to* 8 | REGION: *Sicily, especially Aragona*

Aromatic cinnamon, saffron, cheese, and beaten eggs magically transform into the golden "crust" around this pie. Although it looks showy, it's just a simple process of layering—not at all challenging to make. *Taganu* is a culinary specialty of Aragona, Sicily, and the name comes from the round terra-cotta container in which it's customarily baked. It comes out great in a round cake pan, too.

The recipe dates to the Renaissance, when spices like cinnamon and saffron were reserved for special occasions. Over the years, the locals have followed history's precedent and taken to eating it as part of celebratory meals, and it is most especially associated with Easter.

Preheat the oven to 325°F (165°C). Generously oil a 12-inch (30.5-cm) round nonstick deep cake pan.

Boil the pasta in salted water for half the time the package directs. Drain, toss it with a little oil to keep it from sticking, and set aside.

In a medium sauté pan over medium heat, cook the beef until it no longer red, but not fully cooked. Season it with salt and pepper and set aside.

In a bowl, using a whisk or electric hand-held mixer, beat the eggs with the cinnamon and saffron until combined. Season with salt and pepper.

To assemble: Set aside ½ cup (120 ml) of the pasta and ½ cup (120 ml) of the egg mixture for the final layer. Pour one third of the remaining egg mixture into the bottom of the prepared pan, top with one third of the parcooked pasta, and sprinkle with grated cheese and parsley to taste. Scatter on one third of the cooked meat and top with one third of the cheese slices. Repeat for two more layers.

Top with the reserved pasta and egg mixture. Sprinkle with a few tablespoons of grated cheese. Bake, covered with aluminum foil, for 1 hour, then remove the foil and bake for an additional hour, or until the pie is set and the top is darkly golden.

Let it rest until it comes to room temperature before slicing.

1 pound (455 g) penne, rigatoni, or other tube pasta

Salt

Olive oil

12 ounces (340 g) ground beef

Freshly ground black pepper

20 large eggs

1 tablespoon ground cinnamon

A few strands saffron or 1 tablespoon saffron powder

Minced fresh parsley

Grated aged caciocavallo or pecorino cheese

1 pound (455 g) *tuma* or fresh mozzarella, thinly sliced

PRETTY EASTER PASTA PIE

{ Crostata di tagliolini }

SERVES 6 *to* 8 | **REGION:** *Southern and parts of central Italy*

Homey and comforting, this lovely pie comes together without much fuss. Thin egg noodles are layered with ham, cheese, and mushrooms; tiny peas scattered between the layers add a green burst of flavor. The dish is baked until beautifully golden, sliced like pie, and eaten at room temperature. This is traditionally baked on the day before Easter, to be eaten as part of the family picnics enjoyed on Angel's Monday, Italy's national holiday the day after Easter.

In a small sauté pan, heat 1 tablespoon oil over medium-high heat. Cook the onion and pancetta until the onion is softened, about 5 minutes. Add the peas and a few tablespoons of water, and cook until the peas are tender, about 5 minutes. Season with salt and pepper; set aside in a bowl.

In the same pan, heat 2 more tablespoons oil over high heat. Cook the mushrooms and garlic for a minute or two, until tender. Season with salt and pepper; set aside.

Preheat the oven to 350°F (175°C). Butter an 8- to 9-inch (20- to 23-cm) nonstick springform pan and dust it with breadcrumbs.

In another small pot, make a béchamel: Melt 4 tablespoons (60 g) of the butter over medium heat, stir in the flour, and cook, stirring constantly with a wooden spoon, until smooth. Add the milk and bring it to a boil, stirring until thick, about 2 minutes. Season with salt and pepper. Set aside.

Boil the pasta in salted water for 3 minutes less than the package directs. Drain and toss with the stock.

Layer the bottom of the prepared baking pan with one third of the pasta. Dot with one third of the béchamel, sprinkle it with 2 to 3 heaping tablespoons Parmesan, scatter on all of the pea mixture, then scatter on one third of the diced cheese. Spread out a second level layer of pasta, dot with one third of the béchamel, sprinkle with 2 to 3 heaping tablespoons Parmesan, and scatter on all the mushrooms, ham, and remaining diced cheese. Top with the remaining pasta and any unabsorbed remaining stock, pressing down to compact the layers. Dot the top with the remaining béchamel, Parmesan, breadcrumbs, and remaining butter, very thinly sliced.

Bake for about 25 minutes, until the pie is set and golden. Let it rest until it comes to room temperature before slicing.

Olive oil

1 small onion, minced

2 ounces (60 g) pancetta or prosciutto, minced

8 ounces (225 g) baby peas

Salt and freshly ground black pepper

12 ounces (340 g) fresh mushrooms, any type, thinly sliced

1 garlic clove, minced

About ¼ cup (28 g) homemade breadcrumbs, toasted

7 tablespoons (100 g) butter

¼ cup (30 g) all-purpose or "o" flour

2 cups (480 ml) milk, warmed

1 pound (455 g) *tagliolini*, or other fresh thin egg noodles

½ cup (120 ml) chicken or beef stock

About ½ cup (60 g) grated Parmesan cheese

12 ounces (340 g) *burrata* or mozzarella cheese, diced

8 ounces (225 g) thinly sliced ham, cut into strips

BFF PASTA

{ Tagliatelle Mimosa }

SERVES 4 | **REGION:** *northern Italy*

---

8 ounces (225 g) fresh codfish

3 garlic cloves

2 slices white bread, crusts removed, torn into pieces

Grated Parmesan cheese

1 large egg

1 tablespoon saffron powder or a few strands saffron

Salt and freshly ground black pepper

Olive oil

2 tablespoons butter

⅓ cup (75 ml) brandy, or more to taste

½ cup (120 ml) heavy cream

1 pound (455 g) spinach tagliatelle or other long spinach pasta

In Italy, March 8th is *La Festa della Donna*, International Women's Day. Here in the States, it's not such a big deal, but over there best female friends really do it up—exchanging cards and getting together for lunch or dinner. Because the mimosa blooms in March in Italy, it is the holiday's honorary flower. All day long, everywhere you look, you can spot women carrying little bouquets of mimosas, which are sold or given away on practically every corner.

In celebration of the holiday, chefs and home cooks have created special dishes mimicking the flower's unique color and shape. This recipe is an example: tiny, delicious, saffron-scented fish meatballs served over spinach pasta, meant to resemble a pretty bouquet of mimosas.

In a food processor, grind the codfish and 1 garlic clove until smooth. Pulse in the bread, ½ cup (60 g) of Parmesan, egg, saffron, and salt and pepper to taste. Form the mixture into marble-sized balls.

In a skillet, heat 2 tablespoons oil and the butter with the two remaining garlic cloves until the garlic is golden and fragrant. Discard the garlic, add the fish balls, and cook for 2 minutes, shaking the pan occasionally to rotate the balls. Add the brandy and cook for a few seconds to burn off the alcohol, then stir in the cream and season with salt and pepper. Taste and add more brandy, if you like. Simmer for a few minutes, then remove the pan from the heat and cover to keep warm.

Meanwhile, boil the pasta in salted water until it is al dente. Drain and serve topped with the sauce and fish balls in a pretty cluster to resemble a bouquet of mimosa flowers.

CHAPTER

· 10 ·

Pasta for Dessert

"THE MACARONI HAD BEEN COOKED IN ALMOND MILK
AND SUGAR, AND PERFUMED WITH AMBERGRIS, THE FINEST
GROUND CINNAMON, GENUINE CORINTH CURRANTS, PISTACHIOS
FROM THE LEVANT, LEMON ZEST, THE MOST DELICATE LITTLE
SALAMI, AND GARNISHED WITH MARZAPANE . . ."

Description of a "macaroni pie" that Pere Labata, a French travel writer,
ate in Sicily in the early 1700s.

Italy has a long tradition of serving sweetened pasta like the macaroni pie described above. Back in the Renaissance, pasta was a luxury food, reserved for special occasions and paired with other luxury foods like sugar and cinnamon.

Pictured here are *confetti*—sugar-coated spices, including lavender, cinnamon, and rosemary—which date to the Renaissance but are still served as after-dinner treats in Italy today. Today, throughout Italy, you'll find traditional pasta desserts like Sweet Pistachio Couscous (page 184), as well as many modern creations, including Chocolate-Stuffed Shells (page 182) and Pasta Truffles (page 185).

CHOCOLATE-STUFFED SHELLS

{ Conchiglioni dolci al cacao }

SERVES *4 to 6* | **REGION:** *Northern and central Italy*

---

24 jumbo shells, preferably Felicetti brand

Salt

¼ cup (20 g) unsweetened cocoa powder

½ cup (50 g) confectioners' sugar, optional

FOR THE FILLING:

Approximately 2 cups (480 ml) total of gelato, custard, whipped cream, pudding, fruit, yogurt, etc.

Genius! Jumbo pasta shells coated in cocoa powder and filled with . . . well, anything! Vanilla custard, chocolate pudding, panna cotta, semifreddo, sorbet, granita, whipped cream and fresh berries, yogurt and honey, creamy peanut butter and jelly—there are endless possibilities.

Use just cocoa powder for unsweetened shells that become a gorgeous reddish brown color, or add confectioners' sugar to the cocoa powder for lovely dark-colored sweet shells. I like them both ways! I pair the sweetened shells with less sugary fillings like fresh fruit or dark chocolate pudding.

Boil the shells in lightly salted water until they are al dente and drain.

For sweeter shells, put the cocoa powder and confectioners' sugar, to taste, into a sturdy plastic food-storage bag. Toss the shells, a few at a time, in the bag until they are fully coated with cocoa powder. For less sweet shells, toss them in just the cocoa powder.

Using a teaspoon, fill the shells with anything you like.

A few fun options:

- Ice cream + banana slices + dollop of fudge sauce + chopped nuts = mini sundae
- Ricotta + sugar + mini chocolate chips = soft cannoli
- Mascarpone cheese + sugar + drop of coffee = instant tiramisu
- Cream cheese + fruit jam + fresh fruit = Italian-style cheesecake

SWEET PISTACHIO COUSCOUS

{ Cuscus dolce Siciliano al pistacchio }

SERVES 4 | REGION: *Sicily, especially the province of Agrigento*

Salt

1 cup (175 g) dry couscous

½ cup (60 g) shelled pistachios

¼ cup (40 g) blanched whole almonds

Ground cinnamon

4 to 6 tablespoons (50 to 70 g) sugar

2 ounces (60 g) dark chocolate, grated, preferably Perugina brand

Optional toppings: chopped candied Sicilian squash (*zuccata candita*), dried fruit, pomegranate seeds or other fresh fruit

For centuries, the nuns at the Monastery of Santo Spirito in Agrigento, Sicily, have been selling a couscous dessert seasoned with pistachios. This unique treat, dense like rice pudding, has rich, deep pistachio flavor. It's usually served topped with grated dark chocolate, plus dried or fresh fruit. I especially like adding pomegranate seeds for a pretty burst of ruby red and a tart tang.

In a medium saucepan, bring 1¼ cups (300 ml) water and a pinch of salt to a boil, then stir in the couscous and remove the pan from the heat. Cover and let rest for 5 minutes. Fluff the couscous with a fork and let cool to room temperature.

    Meanwhile, in a small food processor or clean coffee grinder, finely grind the pistachios and almonds until powderlike. Add the nuts and a pinch of cinnamon to the couscous and stir until well combined. Sweeten to taste with sugar. Serve the couscous topped with the chocolate and any of the other suggested toppings.

PASTA TRUFFLES

{ Cioccolatini di fregula }

MAKES *about* 24 *truffles* | **REGION**: *Sardinia*

Fregula, tiny Sardinian pasta, are cooked here in sweetened water, then mixed with melted chocolate and shaped into truffles. They are pleasingly chewy and ridiculously simple to make!

Make them with dark, milk, or white chocolate, or try *gianduia*: dark chocolate blended with smooth hazelnut butter. It's Italy's most popular chocolate flavor and is available online or in Italian food shops. *Gianduia* is delicious, and well worth seeking out (see Sources, page 200).

Bring a small pot of lightly salted water to a boil. Add the fregula and sugar. Cook until the fregula are very tender, about 20 minutes. Drain the pasta and return it to the pot. Add the chocolate and cook over low heat until the chocolate begins to melt. Take the pot off the heat and stir until the chocolate is melted and well combined.

Let the mixture cool enough to touch, then scoop and roll it into little hazelnut-sized balls. Put them onto wax paper and refrigerate until set. Store any leftovers in an airtight container in a cool place for up to 1 week.

Salt

½ cup (55 g) fregula pasta

2 heaping tablespoons sugar

4 ounces (115 g) *gianduia*, dark, white, or milk chocolate, chopped, preferably Perugina brand

SWEET CRISPY PASTA NESTS

{ *Nidi di tagliatelle per Carnevale* }

SERVES 6 | **REGION:** *Tuscany, Sicily, and Emilia-Romagna*

These nests are little bundles of fried pasta popular throughout Italy as a dessert during Carnevale. But they're so quick and easy to make, you can enjoy them anytime.

No boiling needed—just clump a few noodles into a little nest shape, fry, then enjoy. Since the noodles aren't boiled first, it is important that you use only fresh egg pasta, not dried pasta.

You can season the crunchy bundles Sicilian-style, topped with orange zest–infused warm honey and sprinkled with pistachios; or, as they do in Tuscany, using chocolate noodles, drizzled with brandy-infused warm honey and topped with toasted almonds. Of course, there's also the simple Emilia-Romagna style—just topped with confectioners' sugar.

In a heavy-bottomed pot, heat 1 inch (2.5 cm) of oil. Take a few strands of uncooked tagliatelle and loosely twirl them into a nest shape. Fry the nests until they are very light golden on both sides. Drain them on paper towels. Arrange the nests on a platter and serve them drizzled with honey or sprinked with confectioners' sugar, and topped to taste with any of the suggested toppings. Cover any leftovers with plastic wrap and store them in a cool dry place for up to 1 week.

Vegetable oil for frying

12 ounces (340 g) fresh egg tagliatelle, either plain or chocolate flavored

TOPPING SUGGESTIONS:

Approximately ⅓ cup (75 ml) warm honey + orange zest + chopped pistachios + candied orange peel ; or

Approximately ⅓ cup (75 ml) warm honey + approximately 2 tablespoons brandy or almond liqueur + chopped almonds; or

Approximately ¼ cup (20 g) confectioners' sugar + ground cinnamon or cocoa powder

Fritti sono buoni anche gli zampi delle sedie.

———

Fried, even chair legs are delicious.

CHOCOLATE GNOCCHI

{ *Pistum* }

SERVES 4 | **REGION:** *Friuli*

2 heaping tablespoons raisins

2 tablespoons rum

4 tablespoons (60 g) butter

⅓ cup (30 g) assorted minced fresh aromatic herbs including thyme, marjoram, and mint

⅓ cup (65 g) granulated sugar

2 large eggs

4 ounces (115 g) dark or milk chocolate, preferably Perugina brand, finely chopped, plus extra for garnish

⅓ cup (40 g) grated *grana padano*, Parmesan, or other aged cheese

¼ cup (35 g) toasted pine nuts or assorted chopped toasted nuts

2 heaping tablespoons finely minced candied citron or lemon peel

Zest of 1 lemon

½ teaspoon ground cinnamon

½ teaspoon salt

¼ teaspoon freshly ground black pepper

¾ cup (84 g) homemade breadcrumbs, toasted

1 cup (125 g) all-purpose or "o" flour

1 tablespoon fennel seeds

Confectioners' sugar

Sweet gnocchi seasoned with chocolate, nuts, fruit, fragrant cinnamon, as well as hints of cheese, fennel, thyme, mint, and marjoram—this dish has been a Christmastime favorite in northern Italy for centuries. Served warm in a bowl, it makes a delightfully different dessert, perfect on a chilly winter evening.

Pistum, or in Veneto dialect *pastum*, is a term meaning a mix of many ingredients. It has a magic-potion connotation and dates back centuries. Homemakers in the past jealously guarded their secret recipes, passing them down mother to daughter through the generations.

I learned this recipe from Palma, one of the delightful *Cesarine* princesses, who are members of Home Food Italy, an amazing organization of Italian foodies who host dinners in their homes to share the joys of their region's traditional cuisine. They offer a rare opportunity for us American travelers to meet locals, eat at an Italian's home, and enjoy Italian hospitality.

In a small bowl, soak the raisins in the rum until moist.

In a small pan, melt the butter with the herbs and simmer for a few minutes until they are aromatic. Set aside to cool.

In a large bowl, beat the sugar and eggs until light yellow, then stir in the butter-herb mixture, the chocolate, cheese, pine nuts, candied peel, zest, cinnamon, salt, pepper, and the raisins with their liquid. Mix until well combined, then mix in the breadcrumbs. Mix in the flour, a little at a time, until a dough forms; you may have a little flour left over.

Knead the dough until it is uniform and well mixed. Divide it into four pieces. Roll out each piece into a ropelike cylinder about 1 inch (2.5 cm) thick. Cut the rope every 1½ inches (4 cm) to form small nuggets. Press each nugget lightly onto the tines of a fork to make slight indentations. Repeat the process for the rest the dough, setting out the finished gnocchi on a clean cotton cloth in a single layer.

Bring a wide pan of water with a pinch of salt and the fennel seeds to a boil. Add the gnocchi and cook until they are tender and float to the surface, about 4 minutes. Using a slotted spoon, transfer the gnocchi to a bowl and serve them warm, topped with grated chocolate and confectioners' sugar.

COLUMBUS "DISCOVERED" CHOCOLATE

The history of chocolate, beginning with its "discovery," is closely tied to Italy. Chocolate's journey to the Old World from the New began with Christopher Columbus—an Italian. During his fourth and final voyage to the New World, Columbus became the first European to set eyes on cacao beans, which he purchased from the natives and gave to Queen Isabella.

PASTA CANNOLI

{ *Mezzi maniche dolci* }

SERVES 4 to 6 | REGION: *Abruzzo*

1 cup (250 g) ricotta

2 tablespoons sugar, plus extra for rolling

1 tablespoon finely chopped dark chocolate, preferably Perugina brand, or mini chocolate chips

1 tablespoon minced candied orange peel

Pinch ground cinnamon

4 ounces (115 g) *mezzi maniche*, *mezzi rigatoni*, or other short tube pasta

Salt

Vegetable oil

Optional garnishes: chopped pistachios, chopped candied cherries or orange peel, cocoa powder, or chopped chocolate

All the flavor of cannoli, but with a pasta shell instead! *Mezzi maniche*, little pasta tubes, are boiled until al dente, then fried to create a crunchy, tasty container for the creamy sweet ricotta filling. They are a perfect pop-in-your-mouth, one-bite size. I first tasted this amazing dessert in Abruzzo while having dinner with the wonderful Peduzzi family, makers of Rustichella d'Abruzzo pasta.

Try this recipe once and, as it has for me, it'll become one of your go-to desserts. There are lots of ways to vary it. One of my favorite variations is to fill the fried pasta with mascarpone cheese sweetened with sugar and dust it with instant coffee granules and cocoa powder, for a riff on tiramisu.

In a bowl, using a fork, mix the ricotta, sugar, chocolate, candied peel, and cinnamon until well combined. Refrigerate until ready to use.

Boil the pasta in salted water until it is very tender, about 1 minute longer than al dente. Drain the pasta well.

Meanwhile, in a very small saucepan, heat about 1 inch (2.5 cm) of oil until very hot, but not smoking. Add half of the pasta and fry until it is golden and crisp, about 2 minutes. Remove it with a slotted spoon and drain it on a paper towel. Repeat with the remaining pasta.

When the pasta has cooled to room temperature, roll it in sugar, then fill each tube with the ricotta mixture, either using an espresso spoon or by piping it in with a pastry bag. Garnish, if you like, with the suggested toppings. Serve at room temperature.

ALMOND PASTA CRUNCH

{ Torta di tagliatelle }

SERVES 6 | REGION: *Lombardy, especially the province of Mantua*

---

12 tablespoons (170 g) butter

2 cups (320 g) blanched whole almonds

1 cup (200 g) granulated sugar

12 ounces (340 g) fresh egg tagliatelle or other very thin egg noodles

¼ cup (60 ml) almond liqueur, like Disaronno amaretto

Confectioners' sugar

Fresh thin egg noodles tossed with sugar, almonds, and butter and baked in a free-form pile until crisp—this pasta dessert is one of the most famous and popular sweets of Mantua.

Some Italians bake the pasta in a pie crust, but I prefer to follow the advice of locals from Mantua, who believe that a crust just makes for extra work and hides the beauty of this unusual, pretty dessert. You must use fresh, not dried, pasta for this recipe.

Preheat the oven to 350°F (175°C). Line a flat baking sheet with parchment paper and butter it.

In a food processor, grind the almonds and granulated sugar until the mixture resembles coarse sand, then put it into a large bowl with the uncooked tagliatelle. Using your hands, gently toss to coat the pasta with the sugar mixture.

Loosely scatter about one third of the tagliatelle onto the prepared pan in a roughly 12-inch (30.5-cm) round. Scatter the top with 4 tablespoons of the butter, thinly sliced. Repeat for another two layers. Sprinkle the top with the liqueur.

Bake for about 40 minutes, until golden. Serve at room temperature, generously dusted with confectioners' sugar.

CHICKPEA-MOCHA RAVIOLI

{ Calcionetti teramani }

MAKES *about 4 dozen* | **REGION:** *Abruzzo, Molise, and Campania*

Chickpeas for dessert? Yes, you read that right. These uniquely satisfying dessert ravioli, served like cookies, are filled with pureed chickpeas, which create a lovely velvety canvas for the rich chocolate, espresso, and rum. This classic dessert of Abruzzo and southern Italy is traditionally fried, but nowadays for a lighter treat home cooks often bake them instead. They are delicious both ways!

Make the filling: In a bowl, mix all the ingredients until smooth and well combined, then adjust the flavors to taste, adding more of whatever you like. Set aside.

Make the dough: Sift the flour and sugar onto a clean work surface and make a well in the center. Put the wine, 3 tablespoons oil, and the yolk into the well and slowly incorporate the flour. Add about ¼ cup (60 ml) warm water a little at a time, until a dough forms. Knead the dough until it is very smooth. Form it into a ball, wrap it in plastic wrap, and refrigerate for 1 hour.

To assemble: Using about a quarter of the dough at a time so it doesn't dry out and keeping the rest covered, roll the dough into sheets about ¹⁄₁₆-inch (2-mm) thick. Using a cookie cutter, cut out 3½-inch (9-cm) circles of dough. Drop a heaping tablespoonful of the filling in the center of each circle, fold the circles over to create half moons, and pinch the edges closed. Repeat until you've used up all the dough and filling.

In a large, deep pan, heat 3 tablespoons oil over medium-high heat. Add the ravioli and fry, turning them once, until they are just lightly golden on both sides, about 2 minutes. Drain them on paper towels. Alternatively, bake the ravioli by brushing the tops with egg white, placing them on parchment-lined baking sheets, and baking in a 375°F (190°C) oven for about 25 minutes, until they are lightly golden.

Eat the ravioli warm or at room temperature, topped with sugar and a pinch of cinnamon.

FOR THE FILLING:

1½ cups (245 g) mashed cooked chickpeas

2 ounces (60 g) finely chopped dark chocolate, preferably Perugina brand

¼ cup (30 g) finely ground blanched almonds

3 tablespoons rum

3 tablespoons freshly brewed strong coffee or espresso

3 tablespoons honey

2 heaping tablespoons minced candied citron or lemon peel

Zest of ½ lemon

1 tablespoon sugar, plus extra for garnish

Pinch ground cinnamon

FOR THE DOUGH:

About 3½ cups (445 g) all-purpose or "o" flour

1 tablespoon sugar

½ cup (120 ml) dry white wine

Olive oil

1 large egg yolk

Vegetable oil for frying, or 1 egg white for baking

Pasta Glossary:

THE LONG & THE SHORT OF IT

We've been talking about all sorts of things to put on your pasta . . . now, let's talk about the pasta itself. It would take a dozen books to describe the thousands of dried-pasta shapes, then another dozen volumes to even scratch the surface of all the homemade pasta found throughout Italy.

Since I have only this one book, I decided to make it more manageable— I cut the list down to the number of different pasta types you could conceivably try in one adventurous year. In this section, you'll find a photo glossary covering fifty-two unusual dried-pasta shapes—enough to try one new shape a week for a year!

Italian pasta comes in all sorts of shapes, many with adorable, evocative names: elbows, butterflies, bow ties, worms, snails, ribbons, nests, ears, and wagon wheels. And pasta comes in all sizes, from the teeny tiny *pastina* to the gigantic *boccolottoni*.

Regional differences in pasta are both glorious and maddening. Sometimes the very same shape can have two dozen different names, depending on what province or town you find it in. That's why I opted for a visual guide. You may find shapes under several different names . . . but do find them!

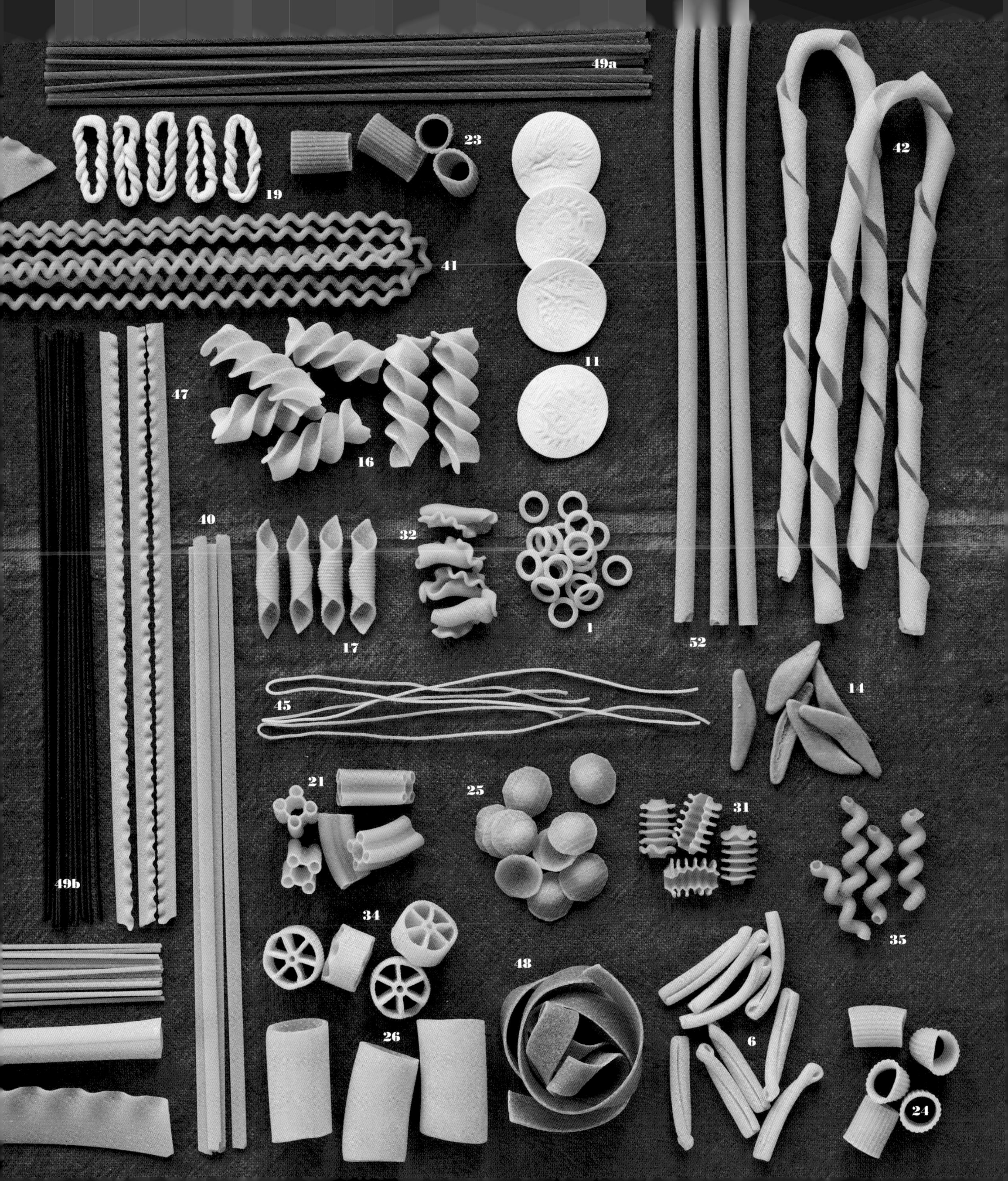

49a

19

23

41

47

16

11

40

32

17

1

52

42

45

14

21

25

31

35

49b

34

26

48

6

24

SHORT

1 | ANELLINI (little rings): great for oven-baked pasta dishes, as they hold together nicely.

2 | BUSA (knitting needles): a specialty of Sardinia, made by rolling the dough around a wooden needle that gives it its name. There are many variations throughout Italy of this type of pasta. In Sicily, a slightly larger version is *busiati*; in Abruzzo it's *pasta al ceppo*; and in other regions it's *treccine* (braids).

3 | CALAMARATA or **CALAMARI** (squid): short, wide ring pasta. Wonderfully toothsome.

4 | CAMPANELLE (little bells)

5 | CANNOLICCHI (little tubes): adorable thin tubes of curled pasta. Often eaten in southern Italy with bean sauces, as in *pasta e fagioli*.

6 | CASARECCE (handmade): made by rolling the dough around a thin rod. A specialty of Sicily, this pasta is reminiscent of *busa*, *busiati*, and *fusilli al ferretto*.

7 | CAVATAPPI (corkscrews): also called *torchietti* (little torches) or even *gigli* (lilies), depending on the maker.

8 | CAVATELLI (carved out): a specialty of Puglia.

9 | CONCHIGLIE AL NERO DI SEPPIA (small shells): flavored with squid ink.

10 | CONCHIGLIONI (large shells): a specialty of Campania, also called *chiocciolioni*.

11 | CORZETTI, CORXETTI, or **CROXETTI**: specialty of Liguria, made by pressing fresh dough between two embossed stamps, leaving lots of grooved surface to absorb sauces.

12 | DITALI or **DITALINI** (little thimbles): small tube pasta often used in soups.

13 | ELICOIDALI (helicoidal): like rigatoni, but the ribbing is more spiraled.

14 | FOLGIE D'ULIVO (olive leaves): their rough texture is wonderful for absorbing sauces.

15 | FREGOLA: a specialty of Sardinia that looks like couscous, and is made with coarsely ground semolina grains instead of flour. The word probably comes from *fregare* (to rub or grate).

16 | FUSILLONI: a spiral of pasta. Also called *fusilli* or *spirali*, depending on length and thickness.

17 | GARGANELLI: a homemade pasta specialty of Emilia-Romagna, le Marche, and Umbria made by rolling the dough around a wooden rod, then pressing it against a special stringed device (called a *pettine*, "comb") that leaves its characteristic lines.

18 | GRAMIGNA (weeds): a curly pasta with a hole through the middle.

19 | LORIGHITTAS (rings): a handmade specialty of Sardinia.

20a | LUMACHE (snails) and **20b | LUMACONI** (large snails): absolute must-tries. You'll love how the sauce sneaks into the hollows.

21 | MACCHERONI CON CINQUE BUCHI (pasta with five holes): a specialty of Sicily served especially during Carnevale with meat ragù. You'll find it freshly made in Sicily with seven or even eight holes.

22 | MALLOREDDUS or **GNOCHETTI SARDI**: a specialty homemade pasta of Sardinia, also found dried.

23 | MEZZI MANICHE (half sleeves): short, thick tube pasta. Often served plated upright. Here shown in a whole-wheat version.

24 | MEZZI RIGATONI (half rigatoni): comes from the word *rigato* (ridged). A smaller version of rigatoni, a specialty of Campania and southern Italy.

25 | ORECCHIETTE (little ears): a specialty of Puglia.

26 | PACCHERI: large tube pasta from Naples, one of my personal favorites—a must-try. Similar are *schiaffoni*, *bombarde*, and *boccolottoni*.

27 | PANTACCE: mini bite-sized lasagne shapes.

28 | PASTA AL FERRETTO (iron pasta): made on a knitting needle or metal rod. Depending on the region, it can also be named *pasta al ceppo* or *ferricelli*.

29 | PENNONI (giant pens): a larger version of penne, fabulously chewy, great with meat and dense sauces.

30 | QUARDRUCCI (little squares): In the past, this pasta was made from the odd bits left after fettuccine were cut. Nowadays, they are made on purpose and served in soup.

31 | RADIATORI (radiators): sometimes packaged as *fisarmoniche* (accordions); also *armoniche* (accordions).

32 | RICCIOLI (curls)

33 | RIGATONI: large tube pasta. The name comes from the word *rigato* (ridged).

34 | RUOTE PAZZE (crazy wagon wheels): thicker and more irregular shaped than traditional *ruote*. Created in 1938 by Puglia's famed artisanal pasta company Benedetto Cavalieri, this shape is wonderful at adhering to sauces.

35 | SPIRALE (spirals)

36 | STROZZAPRETI or **STRANGOLAPRETI** (priest chokers or stranglers): a specialty of the Le Marche and Umbria regions, but popular throughout central and southern Italy.

37 | TROFIE: a specialty of Liguria. The name might come from *strafuggià* (rubbing), the movement used to make them.

LONG

38 | BUCATINI (pierced): also called *perciatelli*, a thick, long pasta with a hole in the center.

39 | CANDELE (candles): over-the-top thick, long pasta, a specialty of Naples. They are broken into pieces and most typically served with Oniony Neapolitan Meat Sauce (page 121).

40 | FETTUCCE: a flat, long pasta, whose name comes from the word *fettuccia* (ribbon).

41 | FUSILLI LUNGHI: also called *fusilli napolitani*. Longer and thicker than short fusilli, but not as corkscrewy.

42 | IANNULATE: also called *sagne iannulate*. A twirled strand of ¾-inch (2-cm) wide pasta, a specialty of Puglia.

43 | LASAGNOTTE: exceptionally long, curly noodles, about 2 inches (5 cm) wide. Festive and fun.

44 | MACCHERONI ALLA CHITARRA: also called *spaghetti alla chitarra*, a specialty of Abruzzo. The dough is cut on a stringed instrument called a *chitarra* (guitar), which shapes the pasta into four-sided strands. Commercially available dried. Shown here in a whole-wheat version.

45 | MACCHERONI DI CAMPOFIGLIONE: very thin pasta from the le Marche region, made with lots of eggs so it keeps its al dente bite nicely.

46 | MAFALDE: broad ribbons rippled on both sides, named after Princess Mafalda. Also called *reginette* (little queens).

47 | MAFALDINE or **TRIPLINE:** a thinner version of mafalde, but with only one side rippled.

48 | PAPPARDELLE: a wide noodle, whose name comes from the Tuscan dialect verb *pappare* (to devour). Shown here in a whole-wheat version.

49 | SPAGHETTI (little strings): Italy's most popular pasta shape. **49a** is flavored with spinach and called *pasta verde* (green pasta); **49b** is flavored with squid ink and called *spaghetti nero di sepia*.

50a | SPAGHETTI LUNGHI: extra long pasta, especially popular during the holidays. **50b | SPAGHETTONI:** a little thicker than traditional spaghetti. Note how some strands show the curved markings of where they were hung to dry.

51 | TAGLIATELLE: a specialty of northern Italy, especially Emilia-Romagna. The name comes from *tagiare* (to cut).

52 | ZITONE: the long version of the ubiquitous short ziti. They can be eaten long, but are generally broken, then boiled and served with thick meat sauces.

Sources

A few of my very favorite Italian pasta companies are:

Benedetto Cavalieri

Felicetti

Garofalo

Giuseppe Coco

Rummo Lenta Lavorazione

Rusticella d'Abruzzo

Spinosi

Online sources for pasta and other ingredients:

AMAZON
www.amazon.com
Carries a wide range of Italian pasta and ingredients mentioned in this book, including saffron powder and *gianduia* chocolate.

ANACAPRI MARKET
www.anacaprimarket.com
A good source for hard-to-find pasta shapes like *crozetti, strozzapreti, maccheroncini di campofilone, trofie,* and delicious farro and kamut-flour pasta from Felicetti. Plus, they carry flavored pastas, including squid ink and saffron pasta, as well as a nice assortment of cheese, cured meats, and other specialty products.

BOB'S RED MILL
www.bobsredmill.com
Sells semolina flour and dried fava beans, which can be substituted for fresh fava beans in Cheesy Ditalini with Fava Beans (page 72) or Apple Ravioli with Fava-Pistachio Pesto (page 156).

CATALINA OFFSHORE PRODUCTS
www.catalinaop.com
A Southern California company that sells very fresh sea urchins for the recipes such as Pasta with Sea Urchins & Coffee (page 138). They ship overnight anywhere in the USA.

DIPALOSELECTS
www.dipaloselects.com
Nice assortment of Italian pasta, cheese, cured meats, and other specialty items, including delicious *mostarda* for Everything but the Kitchen Sink Christmas Tortelli (page 171).

IGOURMET.COM
www.igourmet.com
Great selection of artisanal pasta, including black squid ink pasta, fregula, and other artisanal Italian products.

THE INGREDIENT FINDER
www.theingredientfinder.com
Interesting selection of hard-to-find quality imported products, including terrific Italian chocolate like *gianduia* for Pasta Truffles (page 185).

KING ARTHUR FLOUR
www.kingarthurflour.com

Try their King Arthur Perfect Pasta Blend for any of the fresh-pasta recipes. It is exceptional.

LA FENICE IMPORT EXPORT
www.lafeniceimportexport.com

This California-based company sells incannulate pasta for Pasta with Artichokes, Prunes & Sage (page 40) as well as excellent olive oil and other Italian gourmet items.

LICORICE INTERNATIONAL
www.licoriceinternational.com

Carries quality Italian licorice perfect for Tagliatelle with Smoked Trout & Licorice (page 95).

MARKET HALL FOODS
www.markethallfoods.com

This California-based company is a wonderful source for many fine Italian products, including Rustichella d'Abruzzo pasta. They also make and ship fresh egg pasta. Great inventory of balsamic vinegar, olive oil, gourmet salt, and bottarga.

PENZEYS SPICES
www.penzeys.com

Excellent source for all sorts of spices and specialty salts and peppers.

ZINGERMAN'S
www.zingermans.com

Excellent source for a wide variety of quality imports.

Online sources for pasta-making equipment:

IN THE USA:

AMERICAN-MADE ITALIAN ARTISANAL PASTA TOOLS
www.artisanalpastatools.com

Mr. Terry Mirri, in Sonoma, California, makes lovely hand-carved *corzetti* stamps, *cavarola* boards, *garanelli* and gnocchi boards, rolling pins, and lots of other wonderful pasta-making equipment. He is a true artist and delightful person!
Interestingly, Mr. Mirri was a hot internet topic in Italy last year. Turns out it is very hard to find *cavarola* boards, even in Puglia, where they originated. Word spread online in Italy that . . . gasp, an American was making them! Italians on various forums agreed that in some cases Americans, especially Italian-Americans, maintain the Italian "old ways" more strictly than they do in Italy!

FANTE'S
www.fantes.com

An all-around superb source for all sorts of kitchen utensils, especially pasta-making equipment. Based in Philadelphia, they've got it all: *chitarra* "guitar" pasta makers, ravioli and *cavatelli* makers, *corzetti* molds, Italian rolling pins.

PASTA BIZ
www.pastabiz.com

This California-based company sells home pasta makers, including ravioli molds and the hard-to-find *torchio* for making bigoli, perfect with Duck Venetian Style with Bigoli (page 120).

IN ITALY:

If you are visiting Liguria, it's great fun to shop for gorgeous *corzetti* stamps and visit some artisanal makers such as:

Pietro Picetti in Varese Ligure, Liguria (Via Pieve 15)

Franco Casoni in Chiavari, Liguria (Via Bighetti 73)
www.francocasoni.it

In Piedmont, you can find another version of *corzetti* stamps.

Antica Coltelleria Boido in Alessandria (Via San Lorenzo, 61)
www.coltelleriaboido.it

Acknowledgments

At least 1,000 Italians, and probably more, helped me with these 100 recipes! I can't even begin to list every Italian grandma, home cook, chef, blogger, and friend, so here are just a few that deserve special mention:

Special thanks to the wonderful **PASTA COMPANIES** Benedetto Cavalieri, Garofalo, Felicetti, Rummo, and Rustichella d'Abruzzo—who answered my endless questions, provided recipes and technical advice, and graciously donated their fabulous pasta for recipe testing and the photo shoot. Thanks to Benedetto Cavalieri and his family and to the Peduzzi family of Rustichella d'Abruzzo for their incredible hospitality during my visits. Thanks to Luca de Luca and the team at Garofalo for going above and beyond. Extraordinary pasta, exceptional people.

I am indebted to my gracious **ITALIAN FRIENDS** for arranging pasta-making sessions with relatives and friends and so much more!

Warmest thanks to Roberto Cava and his wife, Valeria Noris, for traipsing throughout Liguria and Piedmont hunting down antique corzetti stamps. Special appreciation to the talented photographer Giuseppe Perrone, of Studio Due in Alessandria, for photographs and to Michele Bottale, President of the Academy of Corzetto di Novi Ligure, who graciously made available his collection of antique *corzetti* stamps.

I can never adequately thank Tiziana Ragusi and her husband, Marco Paolini, for trekking throughout Abruzzo seeking out antique pasta equipment like the gorgeous nineteenth-century *chitarra* they meticulously restored. I will never forget the delightful day of pasta making Tiziana organized, when simultaneously her son, Roberto, her mother-in-law, Margherita Palumbi, and friends Lea Lanciaprima, Marisa Boccanera, Roberta di Donatantonio, and Giuseppina Nallira each taught me to make a different type of pasta.

Special thanks to all 360-plus wonderful Italians affectionately nicknamed *Cesarine*, Princesses, who host meals in their homes for visitors as part of the fabulous organization **HOME FOOD ITALY** (www.Homefood.it). Special thanks to Cristina Fortini and the "Cesarine": Flavia Pantaleo in Rome, Palma in Fruili, Matilda in Lombardy, and Antonietta from Tuscany. A special thank-you to Gabriella and Gianfranco Castaldo, who opened their lovely home and warm hearts to me and taught me the nuances of making Neapolitan Carnevale Lasagne (page 172). Thanks too to Gabriella's brother, Dr. Guido Testai, for the most delicious *pizza fritta* I've ever eaten.

My deepest gratitude to renowned Italian beekeeper Rita Franceschini, from Azienda Agricola Bio in Rome, for all her advice on honey in pasta recipes; special thanks to good friends Luigi Falanga, Febo Cammarano, Marco Novello, and Giovanni Assante. Thanks to my delightful pal and travel buddy, the Italian journalist Sara Scaparone, for advice on Italian food festivals, chefs, pasta makers, and so much more.

I'm indebted to the following **CHEFS** for recipes and advice: Massimiliano Alajmo, of Le Calandre; Carlo Cracco, of Ristorante Cracco; Nicola Portinari, of La Peca Restaurant; Sara Preceruti, of Locanda del Notaio; Niko Romito, of Ristorante Reale; thanks to Gennaro Esposito, of Ristorante Torre del Saracino in Naples, for teaching me how to tell good from inferior pasta; and a big kiss to Davide Scabin, of Combal.zero in Torino, for some of the most unusual, exciting food experiences of my life. Special thanks and hugs to the charming Mauro Uliassi, of Ristorante Uliassi in Senigallia, for all his great cooking tips.

Heartfelt appreciation to Chef Donato Episcopo, executive chef of the lovely Risorgimento Resort in Lecce, for showing me so many fabulous cooking pointers and secret tips. He is a gifted chef and born teacher! Gratitude to Chef Emilio Pasqualini, of Cantina del Picchio, in the town of Offida, for teaching me the 3 Meats, 2 Sauces, 1 Pasta recipe (page 114) and to Chef Gianni Mattera, of Ristorante Alberto in Ischia, for the Mafalde with Mussels in Velvety Chocolate Sauce (page 132). Special thanks to Chef Filippo la Mantia, of the Hotel Majestic in Rome, for the wonderful pestos; Chef Andrea Apea, of Vun restaurant in the Park Hyatt Hotel in Milan, for his inspired Purple Pasta (page 92); Chef Libera Iovine, of Ischia's Il Melograno; Domenico Ciaglia, at Hotel delle Colline in Basilicata; Enzo Barnabei and Maria Gabriella Testa, of Osteria degli Ulivi, a fabulous must-try restaurant in Teramo, Abruzzo; Chef Gioai Miracolo, President of the Italian Federation of Benevento Chefs; Chef Luigi Pomata, of Ristorante Luigi Pomata in Sardinia, and a special thanks to my friend, the wonderfully gifted Fabio Picchi, of Cibreo and Teatro del Sale in Florence. Thanks to the remarkably talented Chef Marco Bistarelli, of il Postale Ristorante in Perugia, for a wonderful dinner featuring five fabulous pasta creations, and to Chef Maurizio Botta, of Vecchia Cantina Baroni in Siracusa, for the delicious Spaghetti in Red Wine recipe (page 87).

Warmest appreciation to these **RESTAURANTS** for help with recipes, local customs, finding food festivals and ingredients, and more: Bar à Fromage Restaurant de Montagne; Osteria 'E Curti; Locanda Al Gambero Rosso; Fornello da Ricci restaurant; Osteria Baciafemmine; Ristorante Centrale di Pirrera Giuseppe; Ristorante Al Becco della Civetta; and Ristorante Il Vecchio Castagno; Vecchia Cantina Baroni. Thank you to La Cecchina Ristorante in Bari, for teaching me all about grano arso, and to Ristorante da Margherita in Elice, Abruzzo, whose pasta alla mugnia and other specialties made for one of the most fun and fascinating meals I've ever had!

My appreciation to these talented **COOKING SCHOOL INSTRUCTORS** for all their help on regional recipes: Giorgia Chiatto and Carmela Caputo, of Cucinamica in Naples; Giovanna Muciaccia, of Insieme in Cucina in Puglia; Valeria Vocaturo, of Cuoche Percaso in Rome; and Rosita Di Antonio, of Teramo.

Thanks to all the fabulous **ITALIAN HOME COOKS** for providing recipes, pasta-making lessons, and lots of advice: Lucia Contrada and her husband, Pasquali Galluccio, for a wonderful day of Pugliese pasta making with the delightful Carla Milone; and Dr. Giovanna Gison and her daughter for the Bucatini Dome (page 74). Appreciation to Anna Moroni, Cristian Mometti, Francesca D'Orazio Buonerba, Pino Correnti, Paolo Cavacece, and Laura Ghezzi.

To **BLOGGERS** Sara Bardelli, Qual Cosa di Rosso blog; Ady Melles, Diario di una Passione blog; Giovanna Esposito, Lost in Kitchen blog; Alexandra Asnaghi, Ombra nel Portico blog; Loriana Ponti, La Mercante di Spezie blog; Virginia Portioli, Spilucchino blog; and Paola Sersante, Anice e Cannella blog. Special thanks to Lydia Capasso, Tzatziki a Colazione blog; and to Maria Teresa Di Marco, Marie Cécile Ferré, and Maurizio Maurizi—a trio of pals with the fabulous La Cucina de Calycanthus blog who all went above and beyond! My gratitude to Sonia Piscicelli, aka "Izn," and her fabulous blog, Il Pasto Nudo, for teaching me the secrets to gnocchi making. A special acknowledgment to

Daniela Dal Ben, Daniela & Diocleziano blog, my go-to for all things Veneto and Friuli, and who deservedly won a contest for her cjalsons recipe; and to Agostina Battaglia, My Pane Burro e Marmellata blog, an invaluable resource for recipes from Calabria. Heartfelt appreciation to ALL my blogger friends, for gifting me with special vintage pasta-making devices, spending countless hours Skyping, answering questions, tracking down recipes, introducing me to chefs, and much more. I cherish our friendships!

Special thanks to Sicilian food historian Dr. Emanuele Lombardo, whose informative Web site, Echo of Taste, is a must for anyone interested in Sicily. On it, you'll find fascinating information and even a novel on Sicily!

Thanks to the many **FOOD FESTIVALS**, but most especially to I Primi d'Italia, a festival held in Foligno, Umbria, every September celebrating Italy's many first-course dishes, and Identità Golose, a wonderful organization that sponsors events around the world featuring the works of Italy's top chefs.

Thanks to the following **ITALIAN CONSORTIUM AND TOURISM BUREAUS** for advice on regional specialties: Raffaele Rossi, of the province of Ascoli Piceno, in the le Marche region; Roberto Pasqualini, of the Pescara province in Abruzzo; Luigi Barbero and the entire team at the Alba, Bra, Langhe-Roero Tourism center in Piedmont; the Grana Padano consortium; Barbara Candolfini and the Emilia-Romagna Bureau of Tourism; Giorgia Zabbini and the Bologna Tourism Board; the Radicchio di Treviso consortium; Stefano Rubino and the Bureau of Tourism for Trento; Walter Santi of Ricette Umbre and the Umbria Tourism Board.

Gratitude and love to my husband, Marc, and daughter, Samantha, for help editing. After so much time spent in Italy speaking Italian, my English prose was left with a thick Italian accent!

Special appreciation to photographer Lucy Schaeffer, food stylist Simon Andrews, talented prop stylist Amy Wilson, and the entire gifted group for all the lovely photos. And finally, my deepest thanks to the entire Stewart, Tabori & Chang team: Leslie Stoker, publisher; John Gall, art director; and my editor, Elinor Hutton, whose sage advice greatly enhanced each and every page.

Index

Index **207**